Apress Pocket Guides

Apress Pocket Guides present concise summaries of cutting-edge developments and working practices throughout the tech industry. Shorter in length, books in this series aims to deliver quick-to-read guides that are easy to absorb, perfect for the time-poor professional.

This series covers the full spectrum of topics relevant to the modern industry, from security, AI, machine learning, cloud computing, web development, product design, to programming techniques and business topics too.

Typical topics might include:

- A concise guide to a particular topic, method, function or framework

- Professional best practices and industry trends

- A snapshot of a hot or emerging topic

- Industry case studies

- Concise presentations of core concepts suited for students and those interested in entering the tech industry

- Short reference guides outlining 'need-to-know' concepts and practices.

More information about this series at `https://link.springer.com/bookseries/17385`.

Governance in Microsoft 365 Copilot & Copilot Studio

Practical Guardrails and Checklists for Secure, Responsible AI at Scale

Suvidha Shashikumar

Apress®

Governance in Microsoft 365 Copilot & Copilot Studio: Practical Guardrails and Checklists for Secure, Responsible AI at Scale

Suvidha Shashikumar
Sammamish, WA, USA

ISBN-13 (pbk): 979-8-8688-2343-5   ISBN-13 (electronic): 979-8-8688-2344-2
https://doi.org/10.1007/979-8-8688-2344-2

Managing Director, Apress Media LLC: Welmoed Spahr
Acquisitions Editor: Ryan Byrnes
Editorial Assistant: Gryffin Winkler

Cover designed by eStudioCalamar

Distributed to the book trade worldwide by Springer Science+Business Media New York, 1 New York Plaza, New York, NY 10004. Phone 1-800-SPRINGER, fax (201) 348-4505, e-mail orders-ny@springer-sbm.com, or visit www.springeronline.com. Apress Media, LLC is a Delaware LLC and the sole member (owner) is Springer Science + Business Media Finance Inc (SSBM Finance Inc). SSBM Finance Inc is a **Delaware** corporation.

For information on translations, please e-mail booktranslations@springernature.com; for reprint, paperback, or audio rights, please e-mail bookpermissions@springernature.com.

Apress titles may be purchased in bulk for academic, corporate, or promotional use. eBook versions and licenses are also available for most titles. For more information, reference our Print and eBook Bulk Sales web page at http://www.apress.com/bulk-sales.

Any source code or other supplementary material referenced by the author in this book is available to readers on GitHub. For more detailed information, please visit https://www.apress.com/gp/services/source-code.

If disposing of this product, please recycle the paper

This book is dedicated to the enterprise leaders, architects, and teams I have had the privilege to work with – those who asked the hard questions, challenged assumptions, and insisted that AI be built with responsibility, trust, and purpose.

It is also dedicated to AI itself: a powerful mirror of human intent, reminding us that governance is not about control but about wisdom in how we choose to build and scale intelligence.

Table of Contents

About the Author

Suvidha Shashikumar is a Principal Solutions Architect at Microsoft specializing in low-code AI adoption, governance, and enterprise transformation. She works closely with Microsoft partners and enterprise customers to design and implement secure, scalable solutions using Microsoft 365 Copilot, Copilot Studio, Power Platform, and Azure AI.

With over a decade of experience in technology consulting and solution architecture, Suvidha has led AI enablement workshops, governance frameworks, and innovation programs across industries, including healthcare, retail, manufacturing, and finance. She has presented at global conferences, coached teams at hackathons, and authored technical blogs and adoption guides that help organizations translate AI capabilities into measurable business value.

Suvidha is recognized for her ability to bridge technical depth with business strategy, making complex topics clear, actionable, and aligned with organizational goals. Her passion lies in helping enterprises harness AI responsibly, ensuring that innovation and governance work hand in hand.

About the Technical Reviewer

Malar Mangai Kondappan is a system architect and integration engineering leader with over 20 years of experience designing cloud-native, API-driven platforms in the insurance and financial services domains. She specializes in turning complex business intent into resilient system architectures, using event-driven microservices, high-throughput data pipelines, and secure interoperability patterns that enable real-time quoting and decisioning at scale.

Her work spans mission-critical quoting engines, external lead acquisition platforms, and end-to-end ecosystem integrations that connect digital experiences, risk platforms, and core transactional systems into a coherent whole. Alongside her architecture work, she actively explores how AI-assisted and "vibe-first" development practices can turn natural-language intent into robust production architectures, closing the gap between whiteboard concepts and running code.

Malar is known for calm, principled leadership: she designs opinionated technical guardrails, mentors globally distributed teams, and brings structure to ambiguity in high-stakes, time-sensitive initiatives. She champions practices that let engineers collaborate with AI tools responsibly using clear domain models, resilient backend design, and iterative feedback loops so that experimental coding styles still result in secure, scalable, and maintainable systems.

Introduction

AI is no longer a future idea. It is already part of everyday work.

It is changing how people write, analyze, collaborate, and make decisions, often with just a simple prompt. But behind that ease sits a more complex reality: access to enterprise data, automated reasoning, and systems operating at scale.

That is where the real challenge begins.

The question today is not whether to adopt AI, but how to do it responsibly, without slowing innovation or compromising security.

This Playbook is a practical guide for leaders and architects navigating that shift. It connects strategy with execution, showing how AI is applied in real enterprise environments using Microsoft 365 Copilot and Copilot Studio and how these tools can be introduced in a way that delivers business value while remaining governed and secure.

AI works best when innovation and guardrails move together.

This Playbook shows you how to build both.

Foundations of AI Governance

As organizations adopt Microsoft 365 Copilot and Copilot Studio, the line between human and machine decision-making blurs. Governance is how you navigate that blur. It's not a policy binder or a compliance gate; it's the intentional design of trust – how you decide what AI *should* do, not just what it *can* do.

In this section, we establish the foundation. You'll explore why governance matters in the age of AI agents, how responsible AI principles translate into real-world controls, and what roles and personas make governance operational. By the end, you'll have the conceptual architecture to build your governance program – anchored in accountability, ethics, and organizational alignment.

CHAPTER 1

Why Governance Matters in the Age of AI Agents

Artificial intelligence is no longer a background tool – it's an active teammate. With Microsoft 365 Copilot and Copilot Studio, AI now drafts, analyzes, and takes action within the very systems that power your business. That level of capability requires clear boundaries. This chapter explores why governance is essential for responsible innovation – how to maintain speed and creativity without sacrificing control, and how to build a framework that ensures Copilot and Agents operate in alignment with your goals, not outside them.

Before we explore the principles and practices of AI governance, it's important to understand how Microsoft 365 Copilot, Copilot Studio, and your organizational data actually fit together.

Figure 1-1 illustrates the core layers of the Microsoft 365 Copilot and Copilot Studio ecosystem – how users interact with AI, where digital teammates (agents) operate, how they are built, and which governance foundations keep everything secure and compliant.

© Suvidha Shashikumar 2026
S. Shashikumar, *Governance in Microsoft 365 Copilot & Copilot Studio*,
Apress Pocket Guides, https://doi.org/10.1007/979-8-8688-2344-2_1

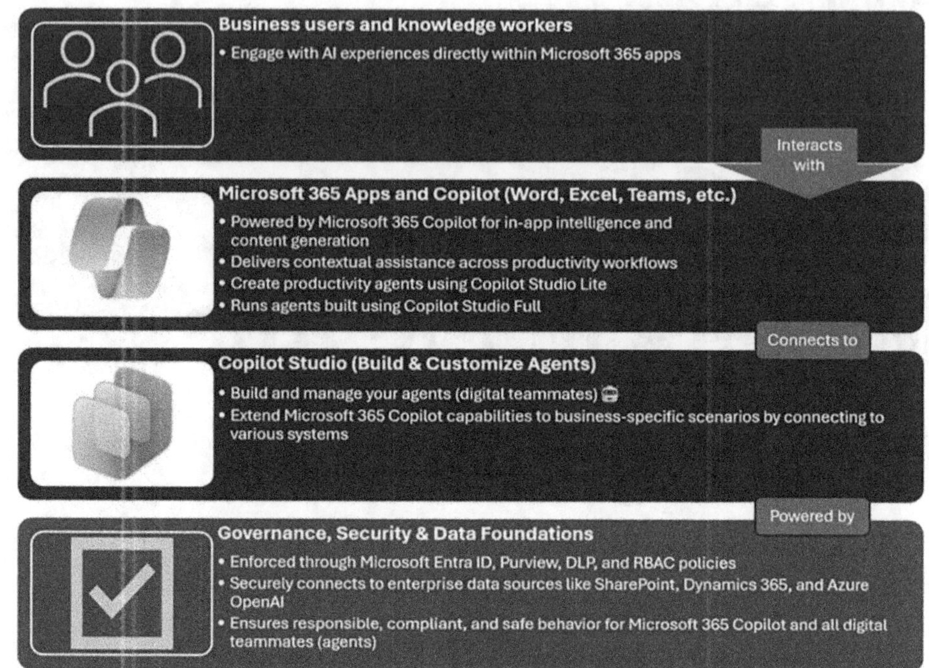

Figure 1-1. Microsoft 365 Copilot and Copilot Studio ecosystem. Business users interact with AI experiences inside Microsoft 365 apps, where digital teammates (agents) run and deliver contextual intelligence. Copilot Studio is where those agents are built and customized. Governance, security, and data foundations power the entire stack, enforcing trust, compliance, and responsible AI behavior

Introduction: The Shift Toward AI-Assisted Works

We're living through one of the biggest shifts in the history of workplace technology. AI has moved from a distant idea to rules-based automation, and now to adaptive, generative systems that can write, reason, summarize, and act. With Microsoft 365 Copilot and the agent-building capabilities of Copilot Studio, that shift finally shows up inside the day-to-day tools you and your teams use every single day.

If you've been in the Microsoft 365 ecosystem for a while, you already know the difference between a *tool* and a *teammate.* A tool waits for your command. A teammate anticipates, suggests, drafts, restructures, and sometimes takes the first step. That's the leap Copilot introduces. You're no longer just clicking buttons – you're collaborating with an agent that can understand your intent and take action with you.

That new power brings extraordinary upside. Copilot drafts your first paragraph, reshapes a spreadsheet, summarizes a meeting you missed, kicks off a workflow, or retrieves insights you didn't know existed. But the moment an agent can reason over your tenant's data, call APIs, interact with Microsoft Graph, or execute actions on behalf of a user, everything changes. You're responsible not only for what the agent outputs – but also for what it *accesses*, what it *infers*, and what it is *allowed* to do.

That responsibility is *governance.*

Governance is how you ensure your AI ecosystem remains secure, compliant, intentional, and predictable – even as agents become more capable. It's how you protect your organization's data estate, earn trust with your users and customers, and create the conditions for responsible innovation instead of accidental chaos.

In this book, I stay practical. You'll understand the controls to configure, the policies to enforce, and the reviews that matter. My goal is simple: help you scale Microsoft 365 Copilot and Copilot Studio agents with confidence – without turning your organization into one big pilot that never quite takes off.

What We Mean by "Governance"

When we say "governance," we don't mean a dusty binder full of unread policies. We mean a living system that enables you to move fast without compromising trust. We'll treat governance as both **design** and **discipline**:

- *Design* is how you shape the boundaries before anyone uses Copilot: which users are eligible, which data is in scope, which connectors are allowed, how environments are structured, and how identities and permissions flow through the system.

- *Discipline* is how you keep those boundaries healthy *after* Copilot is live: monitoring prompts and usage, attesting to access and intent, reviewing drafts, and stepping in when something doesn't look right.

In Microsoft terms, **design** shows up in tenant and environment choices, licensing strategy, Graph permissions, SharePoint site scoping, sensitivity labels, DLP policies, Conditional Access, and which connectors you approve. **Discipline** is reflected in Purview auditing, Copilot usage analytics, cost and consumption reporting, life cycle reviews, and incident response – including revoking permissions or decommissioning agents when thresholds are crossed.

If you do this well, governance doesn't slow you down. It's the runway that lets more teams adopt Copilot, earlier and safer, with fewer surprises.

The Governance Imperative: Your Blueprint for Responsible Innovation

Governance in the age of AI is a strategic imperative that ensures AI works for your organization, aligns with human values, and meets social expectations. As tools like Microsoft Copilot gain the ability to read, summarize, and act across your enterprise systems, the question shifts from *"What can Copilot do?"* to *"What should it do?"*

A strong governance model empowers your organization in four essential ways:

1. **Protect What Matters**

   Define what data is in scope, apply sensitivity labels, and enforce DLP and Conditional Access policies. This ensures agents only access what they need – nothing more.

2. **Build Accountability and Transparency**

   Use tools like Microsoft Purview to log prompts and actions, creating a clear audit trail. Every AI-driven decision can be traced and explained, not guessed.

3. **Set Ethical Boundaries**

   Proactively check for bias in data and prompts. Ensure your Copilot and agents behave fairly, consistently, and in line with your organization's values.

4. **Scale with Confidence**

   Make governance repeatable. With reusable controls and processes, new teams can adopt AI safely – without reinventing the guardrails.

   An ungoverned agent might not break a law today, but it can break trust tomorrow. Your job is to stay ahead of that curve – keeping governance clear, adaptive, and built for a world where digital coworkers are real.

The Risks That Demand Guardrails for Copilot Agents

AI introduces a new class of risks that traditional IT governance models were never designed to manage. We can categorize these into four main areas that directly impact your deployment of Copilot and Copilot Studio agents.

Data Privacy and Security Risk is paramount because Copilot agents thrive on access to vast, often sensitive, corporate data to function effectively. Without strong security and access controls, this fundamental need becomes a major liability. You must ensure that agents adhere to the principle of least privilege – accessing only the data strictly necessary for their task – to prevent breaches and regulatory violations.

Next is **Bias and Fairness Risk**. Models learn from historical data, and if your training data reflects existing organizational or social biases, the agent will replicate or even amplify them. Governance, in this context, requires fairness checks and the use of diverse datasets to prevent discriminatory outcomes, particularly when agents assist in decisions concerning hiring, resource allocation, or customer service.

Then there's the **Transparency and Accountability Risk**. AI decisions can feel opaque. When an intelligent agent summarized a proposal or initiated a workflow, you need to understand how the decision was reached and who is responsible if the outcome is flawed. Governance provides the tools and processes to log, audit, and explain the steps an agent takes, ensuring that its actions are not a "black box."

Finally, **Operational and Reputational Risk** arises because agent systems can fail in unpredictable ways or produce outputs that are factually incorrect. A poorly governed agent can quickly damage your organization's reputation and lead to costly operational failures. Governance ensures robust monitoring, clear escalation paths, and necessary fallback mechanisms are in place.

These risks, taken together, clearly demonstrate that embedding governance is not merely important but an unavoidable necessity for safe AI adoption.

Why Governance Helps You Go Faster

You move faster when people trust the system. We've seen rollouts stall because the first bad demo becomes the only story anyone remembers. A governed Copilot program earns the opposite reputation: "it just works, and when it doesn't, we know why."

Practically, that means you will

- **Start from a clear eligibility model**: Who gets which AI capabilities and why.

- **Launch into environments that match intent**: A safe space to build and learn, a controlled space to pilot, and a production space to operate at scale.

- Keep a short list of "known good" data sources and connectors that teams can rely on without asking Legal every time.

- Offer simple, visible controls to pause an agent, narrow its scope, or adjust its permissions when the situation demands it.

- Show leadership usage, value, and cost in one place.

That last point matters. When you can open a dashboard that ties usage to outcomes and spend, you don't argue about anecdotes – you steer with evidence.

Agent Evolution and the Need for Guardrails

AI agents – like those in Microsoft 365 Copilot and Copilot Studio – are becoming more autonomous. They handle tasks, make decisions, and interact with users. Without clear boundaries, these agents may act in ways that conflict with organizational values or compliance requirements.

Governance ensures that agents operate within defined ethical and operational parameters, are consistently monitored and auditable, and remain aligned with enterprise goals as well as user expectations.

Phases of Enterprise Agent Adoption

Organizations are seeing a three-phased approach in adopting and scaling AI. CIOs should assess agent maturity in the workplace and adjust oversight as solutions become more advanced and widely adopted.

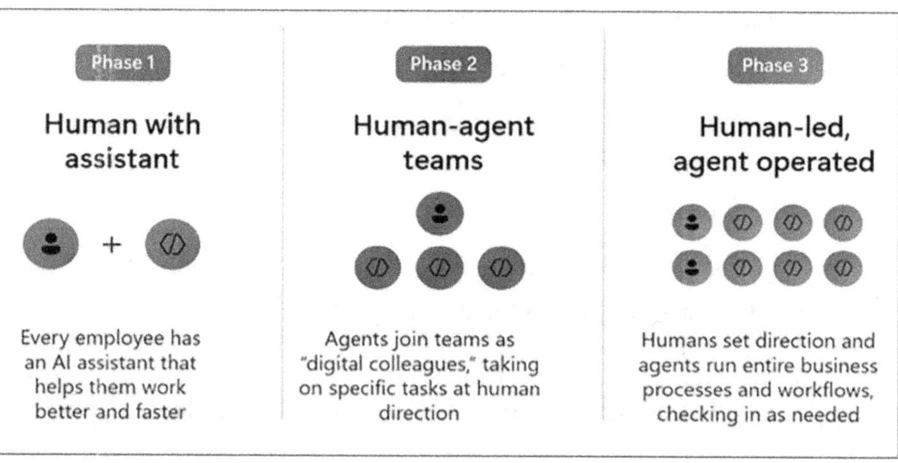

Figure 1-2. *Three phases of the Agent Maturity Curve – showing how oversight must increase as agent autonomy progresses. (Source: The Microsoft's CIO Playbook to Governing Agents in Low code)*

As seen in Figure 1-2, the three phases of the Agent Maturity curve include

> **Phase 1: Human with Assistant**, where agents summarize, automate small tasks, and respond to prompts, such as basic M365 Copilot functions. At this stage, governance focuses primarily on access controls, user education, and initial data flow logging.

> **Phase 2: Human–Agent Teams**, where agents collaborate with humans on structured tasks like data analysis or complete business workflows. Here, governance must define validation methods, compliance checks, and performance metrics.

> **Phase 3: Human-Led, Agent-Operated**. This is where agents take on operational processes with minimal human input, such as a custom Copilot Studio agent managing a service queue. Governance now demands life cycle tracking, real-time permission controls, and treating the agent as "digital labor."

As you can see in Figure 1-2, static controls won't suffice. Adaptive oversight is essential, scaling governance as agents grow more autonomous and complex. This layered approach ensures that the governance framework flexes to the agent's needs rather than forcing it into a rigid, performance-stifling box.

Tiers of Adaptive Human Oversight

Microsoft defines **adaptive oversight** as a dynamic governance model that evolves with agent autonomy. It introduces **three key roles** to maintain control and accountability:

First, we rely on **Reviewers**. These individuals verify the agent's output for factual accuracy, relevance, and compliance before the information is finalized or executed.

Next, we have **Monitors**. They track agent actions and performance over time, triggering follow-up or intervention when the agent deviates from expected behavior or metrics.

Finally, there are the **Protectors**. These individuals or automated systems have the ability to adjust or restrict an agent's permissions, or even decommission it, in real time if critical risk thresholds are crossed.

This multi-tiered model ensures that, regardless of how complex your Copilot Studio agent becomes, a human element is always in the loop, providing the necessary boundaries.

Organizational Readiness: Culture and Leadership

Governance is about more than just tools and processes; it is fundamentally about organizational culture and leadership commitment. For your AI strategy to succeed, you must focus on four pillars of readiness.

First, **Leadership Support** is vital. Executive sponsorship provides the necessary vision, resources, and accountability for a successful enterprise-wide governance framework. Second, you need a **Clear Operating Model**. This means you must decide whether the creation and deployment of AI agents will be centrally managed or distributed across business units, and clearly define the guardrails for each model. Third, **Cross-Functional Collaboration** is non-negotiable. Governance cannot reside solely within

IT or Legal; engaging experts from business domains, ethics, security, and human resources ensures that AI addresses real needs while managing real risks. Fourth, your approach must embrace **Change Management.** AI evolves rapidly, so your organization must prioritize agility and continuous improvement over waiting for a perfect, static solution.

Governance should be your blueprint for safe scaling and resilience, not a barrier.

Key Takeaways

- Governance is not a compliance exercise – it's the structure that lets you innovate safely.

- Treat governance as both **design** (how you set boundaries) and **discipline** (how you keep them healthy).

- Protect data, ensure accountability, uphold ethics, and make controls repeatable.

- The more autonomous your agents become, the more adaptive your oversight must be.

- Culture and leadership matter as much as policy – trust is your fastest path to scale.

CHAPTER 2

Responsible AI Principles in Practice

Every organization wants to innovate with AI – but doing it responsibly is what separates experimentation from leadership. Responsible AI isn't theory; it's the framework that helps you design systems people can trust.

Microsoft defines Responsible AI through a layered model – **from principles to tools** – that guides how governance is implemented across the enterprise. Figure 2-1 illustrates how Microsoft's Responsible AI principles cascade from high-level values to operational tools, forming the layered model that guides governance implementation across the enterprise.

S. Shashikumar, *Governance in Microsoft 365 Copilot & Copilot Studio*,
Apress Pocket Guides, https://doi.org/10.1007/979-8-8688-2344-2_2

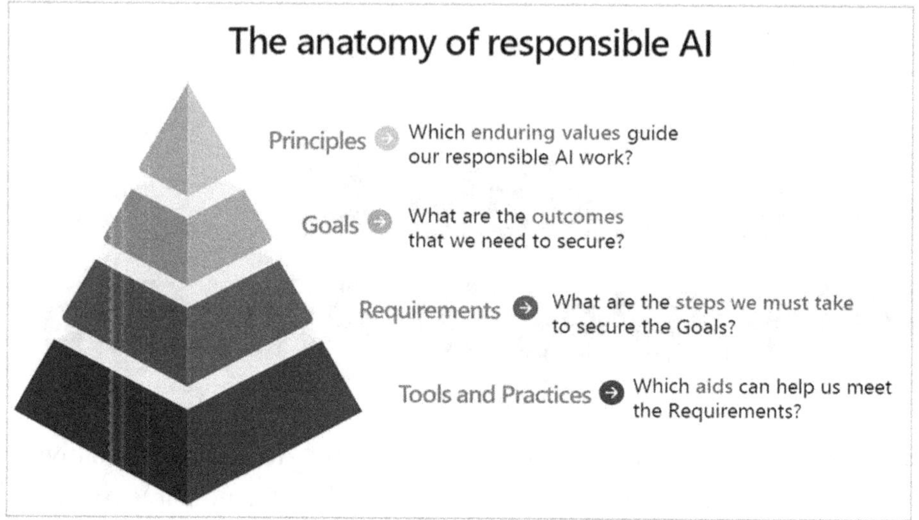

Figure 2-1. *Anatomy of Responsible AI – illustrating how Microsoft's Responsible AI principles cascade from principles to operational tools. (Source: The Microsoft's CIO Playbook to Governing Agents in Low code)*

In this chapter, I'll walk you through how to translate Microsoft's Responsible AI principles – fairness, reliability and safety, privacy and security, inclusiveness, transparency, and accountability – into practical steps for Microsoft 365 Copilot and Copilot Studio.

You'll learn how to configure your environments, control data access, test for bias, document ownership, and create review loops that keep human judgment in the process. These principles aren't abstract – they're the foundation for every governance decision you'll make as you bring AI into daily work.

Building Intelligence with Intention

Every AI system begins with a purpose. You're not adopting AI to impress your organization with cutting-edge technology – you're shaping how people think, decide, and create.

Responsible AI keeps that purpose visible while you build. It transforms broad values – **fairness, safety, privacy, transparency, and accountability** – into daily configuration and operational choices in Microsoft 365 Copilot and Copilot Studio.

When you design with intent, governance becomes an act of design, not restriction. The decisions you make about what data AI can access, who can build agents in Copilot Studio, and how those agents are reviewed, will shape the culture of trust around AI in your organization.

CIOs must define the goal of each deployment. Whether it's reducing manual reporting or surfacing insights, your purpose determines which principles take priority – and which controls must be in place from day one.

Fairness: Designing for Equitable Outcomes

Fairness starts with the data AI can see and use. Because Microsoft 365 Copilot reasons over Microsoft Graph – spanning SharePoint, Teams, OneDrive, and Exchange, you decide which repositories and groups are in scope. If the data is skewed, so is the outcome.

Start by reviewing your sensitivity labels and permissions. Ensure that information across departments, geographies, and roles is represented proportionally. For example, if only one region stores structured project updates, Copilot's summaries will over-index on that region's perspective.

In Copilot Studio, test your custom agents with sample prompts from different user types – marketing, finance, field operations – and confirm the responses remain balanced and factual. Add structured test cases into your ALM pipeline so fairness checks are automated with every release.

Bias doesn't disappear on its own. Create a periodic review where you compare Copilot outputs against known baselines. If you detect imbalance, trace it back to a connector, dataset, or prompt pattern and adjust accordingly.

Reliability and Safety: Engineering for Confidence

Reliability means predictability. When a user provides the same context, Copilot should respond consistently. You can build reliability through configuration discipline: control your data versions, use approved connectors, and separate experimentation from production environments.

In practice, this involves creating **dedicated development environments** in Copilot Studio and enforcing **solution segmentation** through managed environments. Use Azure DevOps or GitHub pipelines to deploy tested versions of agents, ensuring that what users interact with has passed regression and performance validation.

Safety complements reliability. It focuses on protecting people and systems from unintended harm – technical, reputational, or ethical. Microsoft 365 includes built-in safeguards such as content filters, role-based access control, and message tracing. Augment those with your own monitoring:

- Enable **Purview Audit (Premium)** for prompt and action visibility.

- Configure **Data Loss Prevention** to detect when generated content references restricted terms.

- Use **adaptive scopes** to automatically apply compliance policies to newly created workspaces.

Safety also means creating a clear escalation path. Decide who reviews flagged interactions and how corrective actions – such as disabling a connector or adjusting a sensitivity label – are executed without delay.

Privacy and Security: Guarding What Matters Most

Privacy begins with data classification. Label your information before Copilot ever touches it. Use **Microsoft Information Protection (MIP)** to tag files and emails as Confidential, Internal, or Public. Copilot respects those labels, limiting what it can surface in responses.

Apply **Conditional Access Policies** so only compliant devices and trusted users can invoke Copilot. When connecting external data sources or APIs in Copilot Studio, review each connection string and authentication method. Always prefer **Managed Identity** or **OAuth 2.0 with least-privilege scopes** over static keys.

Turn on **Customer Lockbox** and **Data Access Governance Reports** if your compliance posture requires oversight of Microsoft-side access. For organizations under GDPR or similar frameworks, document where data used by Copilot resides and how long it's retained.

Security goes beyond configuration. Educate your users: teach them what it means when Copilot says, *"Based on your organization's data…"*. Awareness remains the most effective security control you can implement.

Inclusiveness: Designing for Everyone

An inclusive Copilot experience ensures every employee gains from AI – not just those in headquarters or with perfect accessibility. Enable accessibility features like **Immersive Reader**, **dictation**, and **screen-reader compatibility** so Copilot outputs remain consumable to all.

During pilot phases, include diverse testers: different departments, seniority levels, and physical abilities. Capture how people interact with prompts and outputs. For instance, frontline staff may prefer brief, actionable summaries, while analysts might need detailed breakdowns.

Inclusiveness also means linguistic and cultural flexibility. If your tenant spans regions, verify that Copilot handles language preferences correctly and that content translation or summarization does not distort meaning. Feedback from global users often reveals prompt phrasing or terminology that needs adjustment.

By designing for inclusion, you build systems that reflect how people actually work – not how the documentation assumes they do.

Transparency and Accountability: Keeping the Loop Human

Transparency allows people to understand and trust what Copilot is doing on their behalf. Document every agent's **purpose, owner, and data scope**. Store this inventory centrally – whether in a SharePoint list, Dataverse, or your governance center of excellence.

Use **Microsoft Purview Audit Logs** to capture when Copilot is invoked, what connectors were accessed, and which user initiated the action. Combine that data with **Power BI** to create dashboards showing adoption, output volume, and exceptions.

Accountability means someone is always responsible for every agent's behavior. Assign an **Agent Owner** role for each Copilot Studio app and include it in your **Data Life Cycle Management** process. When an issue arises – a biased summary, an inaccurate forecast, a privacy incident – you can trace it to a person, a configuration, and a corrective action.

CHAPTER 4

Core Pillars of AI Governance

As Copilot and agents become embedded in daily workflows and when you know who drives governance, the next question is *what holds it together*.

The answer lies in four foundational pillars: **Security, Compliance, Data Management, and Operational Oversight**. Each pillar plays a distinct role, but together they form the architecture of Responsible AI.

These pillars aren't static checkboxes – they're living systems that evolve with every new capability, connector, and integration. **Security** ensures only the right people have the right access. **Compliance** enforces accountability through policy. **Data management** keeps the information ecosystem clean, labeled, and discoverable. And **operational oversight** ensures AI behaves as intended, with continuous monitoring and improvement.

When these pillars work in harmony, governance shifts from being a control mechanism to a strategic enabler – helping innovation scale safely, predictably, and responsibly. Let's look at how to build that architecture, one decision, one control, one review at a time.

S. Shashikumar, *Governance in Microsoft 365 Copilot & Copilot Studio*, Apress Pocket Guides, https://doi.org/10.1007/979-8-8688-2344-2_4

Security – Protecting Access and Identity

Security is the first pillar for a reason – everything else depends on it. Microsoft 365 Copilot operates within the Microsoft 365 trust boundary, drawing from Microsoft Graph, SharePoint, Teams, and OneDrive, and inheriting your existing identity, access, and compliance controls through Entra ID (Azure AD). In contrast, **Copilot Studio extends that boundary**. It allows makers and developers to connect with systems *outside* Microsoft 365 – whether through custom connectors, APIs, plugins, or external data sources. This flexibility unlocks powerful enterprise integration but also expands your attack surface. Every new connector or endpoint becomes part of your governance scope. That's why Copilot Studio must operate under managed environments, where every connection is intentional, authenticated, and monitored.

Start with **least-privilege access**. Every Copilot or agent request runs under the identity of the signed-in user, so permissions in Entra ID determine what data is visible. Review group memberships frequently, eliminate broad "Everyone" access in SharePoint libraries, and ensure external sharing is deliberate and justified.

Next, strengthen **Conditional Access policies** to limit Copilot usage to compliant devices and trusted networks. If users can reach sensitive data through Copilot, their devices must meet your baseline for encryption, patching, and sign-in risk.

For Copilot Studio, **isolate maker environments**. Give creators dedicated development spaces with role-based access to connectors and data. Managed environments and Power Platform security groups provide guardrails so experimentation stays contained and auditable.

Finally, remember that **security isn't a one-time setup – it's a living discipline**. Review access reports and audit logs regularly to detect unintended exposure early. When employees change roles or leave, revoke permissions immediately. Even a single overlooked license can expose sensitive information and Copilot or an agent will treat that access as legitimate unless explicitly restricted.

Security, at its heart, is about protecting trust. When you safeguard identity and access with intention, remaining governance pillars have a stable foundation to build on.

Compliance – Governing AI with Legal and Ethical Boundaries

Copilot and AI agents interact with sensitive enterprise data, which means compliance is not optional. It is the discipline that keeps innovation lawful, ethical, and transparent. Ensuring compliance means aligning your AI programs with legal, regulatory, and organizational standards while maintaining clear accountability for every action an agent takes.

Begin by using **Microsoft Purview Compliance Manager** to map your regulatory frameworks such as GDPR, HIPAA, ISO, or regional equivalents, directly to your Copilot and Copilot Studio deployments. Each control you configure – from retention labels and encryption policies to insider risk management – forms part of your compliance evidence. This evidence demonstrates not only that your environment is protected, but that your governance decisions are traceable and defensible.

Configure **Data Loss Prevention (DLP)** policies and **Information Barriers** to control data movement across departments, tenants, or geographies. For instance, if financial data must remain within the European Union, define rules that prevent Copilot from retrieving or referencing files stored outside that boundary. Purview automatically enforces these controls at the data layer, ensuring that compliance policies apply even when AI systems request or summarize information.

Compliance also extends beyond regulation to ethics. Document how you assess fairness, transparency, and bias within Copilot Studio agents. Maintain an auditable record of reviews, sign-offs, and any mitigations you apply. As global standards evolve, regulators and auditors increasingly expect not just policy but proof that responsible AI principles are embedded in daily operations.

Finally, treat **audit logs** as the backbone of your compliance story. Enable advanced auditing in Microsoft Purview Premium so every Copilot interaction can be reconstructed if needed. When questions arise, being able to show exactly what happened, when, and under whose authority transforms compliance from a defensive task into a demonstration of trust.

Data Management – Owning the Information AI Uses

Copilot and AI agents amplify the quality of the data they access. Poor data hygiene inevitably leads to poor AI outcomes. That is why every governance framework must treat data as a living, evolving asset that requires continual care and oversight.

Begin with **classification**. Use Microsoft Information Protection to label files, chats, and emails based on sensitivity such as Public, Internal, Confidential, or Highly Confidential. Copilot automatically respects these labels and excludes restricted content from its responses, ensuring that data boundaries remain intact even as AI retrieves and summarizes information.

Keep your repositories clean and current. Remove inactive SharePoint sites, archive unused Teams, and apply life cycle policies through Microsoft 365 retention settings. Reducing clutter lowers the risk of irrelevant or outdated content appearing in Copilot answers and helps keep your data estate manageable and trustworthy.

Within **Copilot Studio**, review each data source before connecting it. Confirm that every dataset has a valid purpose, is current, and does not contain unnecessary personal information. If sensitive data is required, ensure it is masked or minimized. Build these evaluations into your environment approval process so that every new data connection passes a compliance and purpose check before activation.

Finally, use telemetry as a feedback loop. Power BI can visualize Copilot and agent usage across departments, highlighting what data sources are most used, which agents generate the most content, and where information overlaps may exist. Visibility into data flows strengthens control, helping you refine your architecture and continuously improve data quality for all AI interactions.

Operational Oversight – Keeping AI Accountable in Motion

Operational oversight is the governance muscle that keeps everything responsive and aligned. Once Copilot and agents are live, governance shifts from setup to rhythm – how often you review, adjust, and communicate.

Establish a regular cadence for oversight. Monthly operational reviews keep attention on day-to-day health, quarterly attestation cycles confirm ownership and compliance, and annual audits provide a structured reset. These checkpoints allow you to evaluate agent performance, retire outdated configurations, and ensure every AI asset still has a clear business purpose.

Monitoring acts as your early-warning system. Combine Copilot usage reports, Purview audit logs, and Power Platform analytics to track adoption, accuracy, and cost. Pay attention to anomalies such as sudden activity spikes, repeated failures, or unexpected new connectors. Patterns tell stories – some positive, some signaling risk, and catching them early is what prevents small issues from becoming systemic.

When incidents occur, manage them through a defined response process. Assign an owner, identify the root cause, document corrective actions, and update your policies accordingly. Closing the loop quickly builds organizational resilience and reinforces accountability across every role.

Operational oversight also depends on clear communication. Share dashboards and insights with leadership and business teams so governance remains visible and collaborative. Transparency turns governance from a control mechanism into a shared partnership between business and IT – one that keeps AI accountable, trusted, and continuously improving.

Bringing It Together

Security protects access. **Compliance** ensures legality. **Data management** defines context. **Operational oversight** keeps it all alive. Together, these four pillars support everything you'll build with Copilot and Copilot Studio.

When one weakens, the others carry the strain. When all four work in balance, governance becomes invisible. It fades quietly into the background, guiding every decision, every prompt, and every action – making sure AI remains trusted, aligned, and effective.

Chapters 6, 7, and 8 are where these pillars turn into actual settings: Conditional Access and tenant controls (Security), Purview and DLP policies (Compliance and Data), and monitoring/ALM for agents (Operational Oversight).

Key Takeaways

- Governance rests on four interdependent pillars: security, compliance, data management, and operational oversight.

- Strengthen security through least-privilege access, environment isolation, and continuous review.

- Anchor compliance with Purview tools, DLP, and auditable processes.

- Treat data management as a living discipline – classify, clean, and monitor.

- Maintain operational rhythm through regular reviews, metrics, and transparent reporting.

SECTION 2

Microsoft 365 Copilot Governance

Microsoft 365 Copilot operates within your most sensitive data boundary. It reads, summarizes, and acts on information that already lives inside the Microsoft 365 trust framework. The question is not whether the platform is secure, but whether your configuration, policies, and oversight are mature enough to manage it responsibly.

As part of this evolving landscape, Microsoft has also introduced *Agent 365* (currently in preview) – a new enterprise catalog inside the Microsoft 365 Admin Center that will unify how organizations view, approve, and manage agents across SharePoint, Copilot Studio Lite/Full, and IT-managed experiences. Agent 365 represents the direction Microsoft is heading: agents treated as first-class digital assets with centralized visibility, metadata, life cycle signals, and governance controls.

This section focuses on the technical and procedural foundations of governing Microsoft 365 Copilot and the agents that extend it. It explores agent types and deployment models, tenant-level controls, data protection and residency, life cycle management, and monitoring frameworks.

You'll see how governance lives in the real tools you already use – Entra ID, Purview, Power BI, and Microsoft 365 Admin Center – and how to transform those tools from static settings into an active, intelligent control system that keeps Copilot secure, compliant, and accountable.

CHAPTER 5

Copilot Agent Types and Deployment Models

Every enterprise wants Copilot to feel seamless – like intelligence built into the flow of work. But behind that simplicity lies a layered system of **agents**, **data**, **connectors**, and **governance decisions** that determine how Copilot behaves inside your tenant.

In this chapter, I'll walk you through how Copilot integrates across Microsoft 365, the types of agents it supports, and the deployment models you can adopt to help you scale responsibly. By the end, you'll have a clear picture of how agents fit within your Microsoft 365 ecosystem – how they connect to data, respect permissions, and scale from pilot to production without losing control.

What Are Agents?

At its core, an *agent* is an intelligent layer that interprets user intent, gathers relevant organizational data, and delivers responses or takes action on behalf of users. Each agent lives inside Microsoft's security perimeter and operates using the same permissions and compliance boundaries as the signed-in user.

© Suvidha Shashikumar 2026
S. Shashikumar, *Governance in Microsoft 365 Copilot & Copilot Studio*,
Apress Pocket Guides, https://doi.org/10.1007/979-8-8688-2344-2_5

You can think of agents as extensions of your digital teammates: digital collaborators that can summarize, draft, calculate, or even initiate actions. Copilot orchestrates a network of specialized agents, each optimized for specific tasks across apps and data sources.

Clarifying the Difference: Copilot vs. Agents

- **Copilot is the user-facing experience**: The interface where users interact with AI to find answers or get help with tasks like writing emails, summarizing documents, or generating insights.

- **Agents are the behind-the-scenes intelligence units that power Copilot**: They are responsible for interpreting prompts, retrieving data, and executing actions. Each agent is tailored to a specific context or task.

In Short – Copilot is the assistant you talk to. Agents are the workers doing the job.

Governance matters because every agent has a footprint – it touches data, interacts with APIs, and influences business outcomes. Understanding the type and behavior of each agent is the first step toward responsible deployment.

Agent Types in Microsoft 365 Copilot

As shown in Figure 5-1, Microsoft defines three primary agent types, each increasing in capability, complexity, and governance need called **Retrieval Agents, Task Agents, Autonomous Agents**.

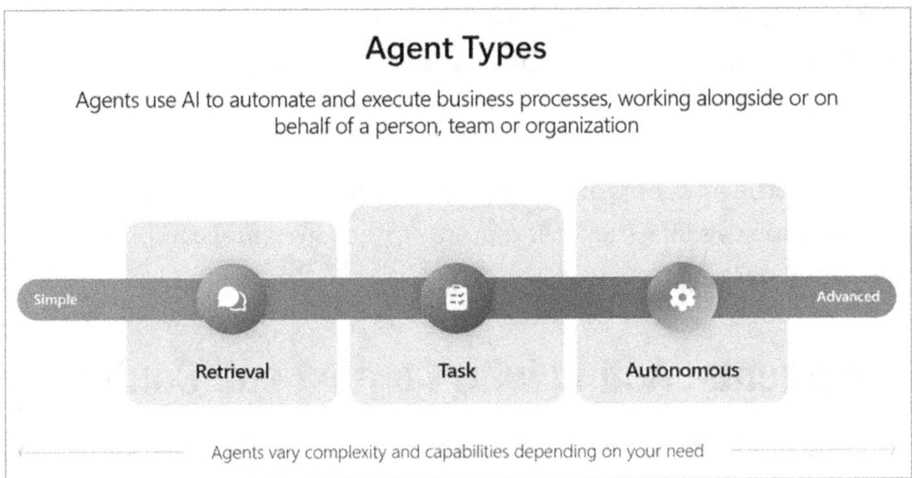

Figure 5-1. *Primary agent types*

Retrieval Agents: Finding and Summarizing Information

Retrieval agents are the simplest and most common. They don't perform actions; they are designed to **fetch and surface information** from grounded data sources (e.g., SharePoint, OneDrive, CRM systems, Microsoft Graph – files, messages, meeting notes, or chats) based on user queries while respecting user access permissions.

You can create retrieval agents using the following experiences:

Copilot Studio Lite in Microsoft 365 Copilot (formerly Agent Builder): Designed for citizen developers, this experience enables quick creation of retrieval agents grounded in SharePoint and tenant Graph content, using a Low-code interface within Microsoft 365.

Copilot Studio: Ideal for makers and developers who want to build agents retrieving data from multiple sources like Graph and third-party services/systems.

SharePoint: SharePoint agents can be created directly inside SharePoint sites or document libraries. These agents are grounded on specific SharePoint content and respect existing site and file-level permissions.

While retrieval agents are generally at lower risk compared to task or autonomous agents, they still require strong governance to prevent unintended data exposure.

Task Agents: Acting with Context and Control

Task agents go a step further. They don't just summarize – they are designed to automate workflows and perform actions on behalf of users. Task agents perform tasks such as submitting forms, updating records, sending notifications, or orchestrating business processes across systems. They are ideal for replacing repetitive, manual tasks and improving operational efficiency.

You can create task agents using

Copilot Studio: Ideal for makers and developers. Copilot Studio provides a Low-code interface to design task agents with Tools to connect with Microsoft 365, Power Platform and third-party services/systems and Workflows to automate multi-step processes.

SharePoint: SharePoint agents are best suited for lightweight, content-driven tasks within SharePoint sites and libraries. These agents do not support external connectors or orchestration.

Task agents introduce moderate governance complexity due to their ability to act on behalf of users and interact with enterprise systems.

Autonomous Agents: Operating on Behalf of Users

Autonomous agents represent the most advanced category of agents. Unlike retrieval or task agents, autonomous agents are designed to operate with minimal human input, initiating actions, making decisions, and orchestrating multi-step workflows across systems. These agents act as **digital coworkers**, capable of managing complex processes end-to-end.

Imagine an agent that monitors an inbox for contract requests, drafts a response, routes it for approval, and schedules follow-up meetings – all automatically. They are ideal for scenarios where **speed, consistency, and scale** are critical, such as customer service automation, compliance workflows, or operational triage.

You can create autonomous agents using

Copilot Studio: Makers and developers use tools, workflows, and orchestration logic to design agents that interact with multiple systems, including Microsoft Graph, and third-party APIs.

Autonomous agents require the most rigorous governance due to their complexity and potential impact. Designing them demands robust discipline, including clearly defined boundaries, fallback mechanisms, and human-in-the-loop checkpoints to ensure safe and accountable operation.

Governance Across the Spectrum of Agents

As agents evolve from **Retrieval** to **Task** to **Autonomous**, governance must scale in depth and complexity. Each agent type introduces unique risks and operational behaviors, requiring tailored controls. However, a unified governance framework ensures consistency, compliance, and adaptability across all agent types, including SharePoint agents.

Core Governance Principles for All Agent Types

Regardless of type, all agents must adhere to foundational governance pillars:

Access Control: Agents must only surface or act on data users are authorized to access. Oversharing at the data layer (e.g., permissive SharePoint or Teams permissions) can lead to unintended exposure.

Sensitivity Labels and DLP: Microsoft Purview sensitivity labels and Data Loss Prevention (DLP) policies must be enforced. Agents will not process or surface content that violates these policies.

Audit and Monitoring: Use Microsoft Purview audit logs to track agent interactions. All agents, including .agent files in SharePoint, inherit file-level permissions and life cycle policies. Admins can monitor usage via Microsoft 365 Admin Center (MAC), Power Platform Admin Center (PPAC), and SharePoint site statistics.

Environment Isolation: Use managed environments and environment routing in Power Platform Admin Center to separate development, testing, and production agents. This applies to agents built using Copilot Studio.

Agent Inventory and Life Cycle: Maintain visibility into agent metadata, usage, and ownership. Agents can be blocked, retired, or reassigned using Microsoft 365 Admin Center (MAC) and Power Platform Admin Center (PPAC). SharePoint agents behave like files and follow standard life cycle policies (e.g., retention, archival, deletion).

Scaling Governance: From Task to Autonomous Agents

As agents evolve from executing single-step actions to making autonomous decisions, governance must strengthen across five domains: Access, Oversight, Data Protection, Compliance, and Life cycle.

Role-Based Access Control (RBAC): Assign maker and user roles precisely, restricting environment access via PPAC. Grant privileges only to approved creators and maintain separation of duties between makers, reviewers, and administrators.

Connector and API Governance: Apply DLP policies to control connector usage (e.g., SQL, Outlook, SharePoint) and restrict risky write operations. Use connector classification (Business, Non-Business, Blocked) to prevent unauthorized data flows.

Telemetry and Alerts: Use Microsoft Sentinel and Azure Monitor for real-time monitoring and anomaly detection. Implement alert thresholds for unauthorized actions, unexpected data access, or behavior drift.

Life Cycle and Deployment Management: Implement ALM pipelines with approvals, version control, and safe deployment paths. Include agent attestation and quarterly reviews to validate ongoing business relevance and compliance.

Billing and Capacity Planning: Track consumption and set usage alerts in PPAC. Allocate message capacity strategically and monitor usage trends for optimization.

eDiscovery and Compliance: Ensure all agent interactions are logged and discoverable. Use Purview for audit, eDiscovery, and communication compliance to support legal and regulatory requirements.

Insider Risk and Behavioral Monitoring: Detect risky prompts, unauthorized actions, or data exfiltration attempts using Purview Insider Risk Management and Microsoft Defender alerts.

Adaptive Oversight and Human-in-the-Loop: For autonomous agents, define clear autonomy levels and fail-safe triggers. Use tiered authorization so higher-risk operations require human approval.

Identity and Life Cycle Management: Treat autonomous agents as digital colleagues – assign unique identities, apply conditional access policies, and include them in joiner/mover/leaver and life cycle governance processes.

Continuous Governance and Feedback Loop: Governance should operate as a living system – continuously evaluating agent performance, compliance, and ethical boundaries through Center of Excellence (CoE) reviews and attestation cycles.

SharePoint Agents: Governed by Content, Not Code

SharePoint agents are a unique category of Copilot agents created directly within SharePoint sites and document libraries. These agents have no access to external connectors or orchestration – only grounded content within SharePoint. SharePoint agents are governed as files – meaning their behavior, access, and life cycle are tied to SharePoint's existing content governance model.

Governance Characteristics of SharePoint agents include

> **Permission Inheritance**: SharePoint agents inherit permissions from the site or library they reside in. If a user can access the .agent file, they can invoke the agent. This makes **SharePoint permissions and sensitivity labels** the primary governance mechanism.

> **Restricted Access Control (RAC)**: Admins can apply RAC policies to limit who can view or run agents, even within shared sites.

> **Restricted Content Discovery (RCD)**: RCD ensures agents don't surface content from libraries or folders that users shouldn't discover – even if they have indirect access.

> **Life Cycle Management**: Agents are treated like documents. You can apply retention labels, archive policies, and deletion schedules using Microsoft Purview and SharePoint Advanced Management.

> **Audit and Monitoring**: Agent usage is logged via SharePoint site analytics and Microsoft Purview audit logs. This includes who invoked the agent, what content was accessed, and what actions were taken.

While SharePoint agents are simpler to deploy, they still demand disciplined governance. Maintaining good content hygiene is essential – poorly labeled or overly permissive libraries can result in unintentional oversharing. Every agent should have a clearly defined owner responsible for its scope, maintenance, and compliance posture. Regular attestation and review cycles should include SharePoint agents to confirm that they remain relevant, secure, and aligned with organizational data governance standards. Consistent oversight ensures that even the simplest agents operate safely within enterprise boundaries while contributing meaningfully to productivity and collaboration.

Agent 365 (Preview) – Centralized Visibility and Monitoring

Microsoft Agent 365, currently in preview, is the enterprise control plane for managing AI agents across Microsoft 365. It provides a unified dashboard for visibility, governance, and life cycle management of agents built with Copilot Studio (lite and full), custom engine frameworks, and more. Agent 365 delivers observability through telemetry and analytics, supports advanced search and filtering, and enforces security and compliance via identity and access controls. It also offers insights into usage and billing for metered agents, helping organizations optimize resources and maintain compliance.

Agent Life Cycle Management and Versioning

As agents become embedded in enterprise workflows, managing their life cycle is no longer optional, it's essential. Governance must extend beyond deployment to include how agents evolve, retire, and remain accountable over time.

Life Cycle Stages

Agents should be treated as digital assets with a defined life cycle:

Design and Build: Created in governed environments with documented purpose and scope.

Test and Validate: Reviewed for reliability, fairness, and compliance before going live.

Deploy and Monitor: Published to production environments with telemetry and audit logging enabled.

Review and Update: Subject to quarterly attestation cycles to confirm continued relevance and safety.

Retire or Reassign: Decommissioned when obsolete or reassigned if ownership changes.

Version control is integral to this rhythm. Application Life Cycle Management pipelines, managed through Azure DevOps or GitHub, ensure consistent rollouts, rollback mechanisms, and regression testing before updates are approved.

Each agent must also have a clearly documented owner. Centralizing ownership metadata – including purpose, data scope, connectors used, and last review date – creating visibility and accountability across the organization.

Life cycle governance thrives on rhythm. Monthly operational reviews surface performance trends and anomalies. Quarterly attestation cycles confirm ownership, relevance, and policy alignment. Annual audits assess compliance and strategic fit, ensuring that the agent portfolio evolves with business and regulatory demands.

As agents become more autonomous, life cycle governance must mature as well. Instead of static tiering based solely on risk, organizations can adopt a zoned governance approach, adjusting oversight based on operational context, data sensitivity, and level of autonomy. This adaptive model allows governance to scale intelligently – tight where risk is high, flexible where innovation requires freedom.

For a comprehensive framework on implementing zoned governance across Microsoft 365 Copilot and Copilot Studio, refer to Chapter 9.

Key Takeaways

- Agents operate within user permissions and data boundaries, and fall into three categories: retrieval, task, and autonomous – each requiring progressively stronger governance.

- Governance must scale with agent complexity, using access controls, sensitivity labels, DLP policies, audit logs, environment isolation, and agent inventories.

- Life cycle management is critical, with governance applied from design through retirement using ALM pipelines, attestation cycles, and ownership metadata.

- Risk classification helps tailor governance strategies, with agents grouped into zoned governance tiers based on their capabilities and impact.

CHAPTER 6

Tenant Controls, Permissions, and Licensing Strategy

Governance Starts at the Tenant Level. Before Copilot can operate effectively, organizations must establish a secure and compliant foundation within their Microsoft 365 tenant. The tenant acts as the **control surface**, defining how Copilot behaves, who can use it, and what data it can access. This chapter walks through those controls so you can enable Copilot deliberately, not by default.

The Tenant As Your Control Plane

Your Microsoft 365 tenant defines the boundary of trust. Copilot does not create a new identity or bypass your existing security model. It functions entirely within the Microsoft 365 perimeter, governed by Entra ID, Microsoft Graph, and the compliance and data protection policies you have already configured in Purview.

© Suvidha Shashikumar 2026
S. Shashikumar, *Governance in Microsoft 365 Copilot & Copilot Studio*,
Apress Pocket Guides, https://doi.org/10.1007/979-8-8688-2344-2_6

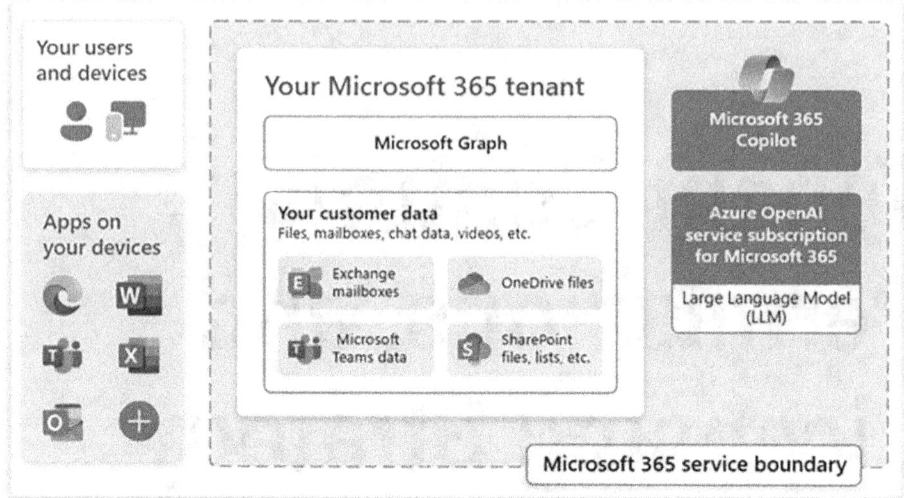

Figure 6-1. *Microsoft 365 service boundary*

As seen in Figure 6-1, Copilot operates within your Microsoft 365 service boundary.

All requests flow through Microsoft Graph, respecting existing security, compliance, and data-access controls defined in your tenant.

Every Copilot request runs in the context of the signed-in user's identity, accessing only what that user is already permitted to see. This means your existing Zero Trust practices like verify explicitly, use least privilege, and assume breach – still apply.

Tenant-level governance is about removing assumptions and reinforcing clarity. Review who has permission to create sites, share content externally, or connect third-party data sources. The fewer unknowns that exist in your tenant configuration, the easier it becomes to predict Copilot's behavior and maintain consistent control.

Configuring Tenant-Level Controls

Tenant-level controls determine how far Copilot can reach and how safely it operates. When configured well, tenant controls create a balance between innovation and discipline. They allow users to explore AI capabilities with confidence, knowing that every action still sits within the organization's security, compliance, and data boundaries.

Start by aligning your configuration with three priorities: secure data access, compliance enforcement, and monitoring readiness. Security defines what Copilot can reach. Compliance determines what it is allowed to process. Monitoring ensures that every interaction remains observable and accountable. Together, these priorities form the control surface for all Copilot activity in your Microsoft 365 tenant.

Central Administration Through the Microsoft 365 Admin Center

The Microsoft 365 Admin Center (MAC) serves as the central point of administration for Copilot and other Microsoft 365 services. From here, administrators can control which workloads – Word, Excel, Teams, PowerPoint, Outlook, Loop, or Whiteboard – are Copilot-enabled, assign licenses, and manage integrated applications.

Each agent or Copilot experience appears in the Integrated Apps section, which now functions as the tenant's central *agent catalog*. Administrators can see every approved, pending, or blocked agent along with its permissions, data access scopes, connector usage, and publisher attestation details. This visibility helps ensure only trusted and compliant agents operate in the tenant, preventing shadow agents or redundant functionality from proliferating.

This is also where the **Copilot Control System (CCS)** comes into play. CCS is Microsoft's unified governance framework for Copilot – bringing together security and governance, management controls, and measurement and reporting into a single operating model. While Integrated Apps provides the control surface, CCS provides the strategy behind it:

- **Security and governance**: How Copilot accesses, processes, and protects organizational data.

- **Management controls**: Approvals, app/agent life cycle, usage boundaries, and policy enforcement.

- **Measurement and reporting**: Adoption, usage trends, productivity insights, and readiness metrics.

MAC surfaces many of these CCS controls directly – letting administrators track usage, restrict or unblock agents, run controlled pilots, and enforce consistent policies across the tenant. As your Copilot deployment grows, CCS becomes the lens through which you interpret these settings and ensure responsible scaling.

Tenant configuration, when managed deliberately, becomes more than an IT function – it becomes the governance heartbeat of your Copilot ecosystem, shaping how AI interacts with your people, your processes, and your data.

Identity, Data, and Monitoring Controls

Tenant-level governance begins with identity. Every control, from access permissions to data handling, depends on how securely users authenticate and how consistently those identities are verified. Microsoft Entra ID provides the foundation for that trust. It defines the authentication, authorization, and device compliance rules that Copilot obeys.

Multi-factor authentication, conditional access, and session controls ensure that only verified users on managed and compliant devices can interact with organizational data through Copilot. Administrators can further strengthen protection by aligning Entra ID policies with Microsoft Purview sensitivity labels. For example, you can require managed devices for documents labeled "Highly Confidential" or block external sessions from accessing sensitive data. This connection between identity and labeling creates a continuous loop of trust.

Once identity is secured, data protection defines what Copilot can discover and reference. SharePoint Online and OneDrive remain the gatekeepers for content, while Microsoft Purview governs classification, labeling, and protection. SharePoint Advanced Management adds another layer of precision with tools such as Restricted Content Discovery, which hides specific sites or libraries from Copilot indexing, and site-sharing restrictions that prevent oversharing.

Microsoft Purview Information Protection applies sensitivity labels consistently across SharePoint, Teams, and Outlook. These labels automatically inform Copilot's behavior, ensuring that files marked "Highly Confidential" are excluded from results while general content remains available. Data Loss Prevention policies reinforce these safeguards by scanning for sensitive information – such as credentials, personal data, or financial details – and blocking access or alerting compliance teams when violations occur. Together, these configurations form the tenant's data governance backbone.

Monitoring closes the loop. Every Copilot interaction within the tenant is logged in Microsoft Purview Audit, creating a traceable record of who accessed what, when, and through which context. These logs integrate with eDiscovery to support investigations and compliance reviews. For deeper insights, administrators can extend monitoring with Microsoft Sentinel, using its analytics and automation capabilities to correlate

Copilot activity with broader security events. Sentinel transforms audit data into actionable intelligence, helping you detect anomalies early and verify that governance policies are being followed in real time.

Identity, data, and monitoring controls work best as a single ecosystem. Identity determines who can act, data protection defines what they can reach, and monitoring confirms that every action stays within policy. When these layers operate in unison, the tenant evolves from a configuration boundary into a living governance framework which is secure, adaptive, and verifiable.

Operational Governance

Tenant controls define the technical perimeter, but governance only succeeds when people actively uphold it. Even the most secure configuration depends on how teams manage access, maintain permissions, and handle data in daily practice. Operational governance turns technical policy into living behavior – it is what keeps Copilot secure as projects evolve, teams expand, and data boundaries shift.

Operational governance begins with ownership. Every environment, site, and Copilot experience should have a clearly identified steward responsible for its configuration, compliance, and review. The Global Administrator oversees overall enablement and policy settings, while Entra ID administrators manage authentication, multifactor access, and device compliance. Purview administrators handle sensitivity labels, data loss prevention, and life cycle policies. At the content layer, site owners and information stewards control permissions and sharing settings. Together, these roles create a chain of accountability that connects tenant governance to real-world execution.

Access reviews are the heartbeat of this stewardship model. Permissions naturally drift over time as roles change and projects close. Regular reviews confirm that users still need the access they hold and that sensitivity labels remain accurate. Microsoft 365 automates much of this process by prompting site owners to validate memberships and content relevance. Workspaces or libraries that remain inactive or unattested can be archived or removed, keeping the tenant lean and reducing exposure.

Purview audit logs extend this discipline by recording every Copilot interaction, giving administrators visibility into how AI is being used across the organization. These records integrate with eDiscovery and Sentinel dashboards, closing the feedback loop between oversight and operational activity.

Finally, governance culture matters as much as configuration. The principle of least privilege should shape every access decision. Users should have only what they need and only for as long as it serves a legitimate purpose. When this mindset becomes part of onboarding, reviews, and leadership communication, governance stops being a periodic task and becomes a shared value.

Operational governance and stewardship ensure that your technical controls are not static settings but living commitments. They make compliance continuous, access intentional, and Copilot trustworthy by design.

Licensing Strategy and Cost Management

Licensing is both a control and a commitment. Assigning Copilot access defines who can use the technology, how costs accumulate, and how data governance policies apply. A clear licensing strategy allows administrators to balance innovation with accountability, ensuring that Copilot is introduced where it delivers measurable value.

Licenses should never be treated as an entitlement. Each one represents an operational boundary that connects an identity, a compliance policy, and a budget line. Assigning licenses intentionally reinforces both security and fiscal discipline while supporting the organization's AI adoption journey. When licensing aligns with identity governance, cost management becomes a natural extension of security and compliance.

Licensing Models and Consumption Strategy

Microsoft 365 Copilot can be licensed through either per-user or consumption-based models, depending on organizational maturity and scale. Most enterprises begin with per-user licensing, typically tied to Microsoft 365 E3 or E5 subscriptions (make sure to check Microsoft licensing guide for up-to-date information). This approach provides predictable costs and allows administrators to define exactly who has access to Copilot experiences.

When planning distribution, start small. Introduce Copilot to controlled pilot groups such as productivity champions, power users, or departments with well-defined use cases. Gather adoption feedback, evaluate productivity gains, and refine governance controls before expanding across the organization. This deliberate rollout validates configuration, mitigates risk, and builds internal confidence.

For flexible or short-term scenarios, administrators can choose a pay-as-you-go model for Copilot Chat or agent-based experiences. Consumption licensing tracks actual usage rather than fixed seats, making it ideal for proofs of concept, seasonal workloads, or projects that require limited access. It supports experimentation without long-term cost commitments while still respecting identity and compliance boundaries.

Regardless of the model, licensing must align with governance. Licenses should map directly to active identities in Entra ID, and deprovisioned users must automatically lose Copilot access. Administrators should regularly review usage reports and spending trends within the Microsoft 365 or Power Platform Admin Center to ensure that financial and operational governance remain synchronized.

Licensing decisions should remain in sync with Conditional Access and identity policies defined at the tenant level, ensuring that only verified users on trusted devices can use their assigned Copilot privileges.

Licensing is not a billing exercise – it is a control point that defines who can interact with AI in the enterprise and under what circumstances.

Tracking Utilization and Avoiding Sprawl

Once licenses are assigned, administrators must ensure that Copilot access is being used effectively and that inactive allocations are reclaimed. Tracking utilization is essential to maintaining both financial efficiency and operational control.

The Microsoft 365 Admin Center provides detailed analytics, including usage trends, adoption reports, and per-user activity summaries. These insights help you identify where Copilot is delivering measurable value and where licenses may be underused. Regular reviews prevent silent sprawl – situations where licenses remain active but contribute little to productivity or insight.

Conduct periodic audits to identify accounts with minimal or no activity. Reclaiming or reassigning those licenses not only reduces unnecessary cost but also sharpens visibility into who is actively engaging with AI tools. Integrating license data with Purview Audit or Microsoft Sentinel dashboards can further enhance visibility, allowing you to correlate usage metrics with compliance posture and security signals.

Effective utilization tracking turns licensing into a dynamic governance tool. It ensures that every license serves a purpose, every cost supports value, and every Copilot instance operates within a monitored, intentional framework. The goal is not to maximize license counts but to optimize them for meaningful use across the enterprise.

Key Takeaways

- **Governance begins at the tenant:** Your Microsoft 365 tenant defines Copilot's trust boundary. Every request runs in the user's identity context, inheriting existing security, compliance, and access controls.

- **The Microsoft 365 Admin Center is the control hub:** Use it to manage Copilot settings, integrated apps, and usage analytics. Centralized control ensures only approved agents and workloads operate within the tenant.

- **Identity and Conditional Access enforce trust:** Entra ID policies, multi-factor authentication, and session controls determine who can use Copilot and under what conditions. Align these rules with data sensitivity to maintain a closed loop of trust.

- **Data protection depends on consistent labeling:** Sensitivity labels, Data Loss Prevention (DLP), and SharePoint Advanced Management keep Copilot grounded in secure and compliant content. What a user cannot open, Copilot cannot reveal.

- **Governance is sustained by people:** Clear roles for Global, Entra ID, and Purview administrators – along with regular access reviews – turn security policy into daily practice.

- **Licensing is part of governance, not just procurement:** Assign licenses deliberately, monitor usage, and reclaim inactive allocations to balance innovation with fiscal discipline.

CHAPTER 7

Data Protection and Life Cycle Governance

As Copilot becomes woven into everyday work, governance must shift from configuration to care. Security defines who can access data, but data protection defines how that data behaves once accessed. Life cycle governance, meanwhile, ensures that agents remain accurate, compliant, and valuable as they evolve over time. Together, these disciplines protect not only information but also trust – the core currency of intelligent systems.

Data Classification and Sensitivity Labels

Data protection begins with clarity. You cannot protect what you have not defined.

Use **Microsoft Purview Information Protection (MIP)** within the **Purview Compliance Portal** to classify and label data according to its sensitivity as *public, internal, confidential, or highly confidential*. Copilot automatically honors these labels, showing only what a user's permissions and data classification allow.

For example, a document labeled *Highly Confidential – Financial* will never appear in Copilot results for a marketing user, even if that user has access to the containing SharePoint site.

© Suvidha Shashikumar 2026

S. Shashikumar, *Governance in Microsoft 365 Copilot & Copilot Studio*, Apress Pocket Guides, https://doi.org/10.1007/979-8-8688-2344-2_7

Apply labeling consistently across SharePoint, Teams, Outlook, and OneDrive. Each label should trigger appropriate protective action, such as encryption, watermarking, or access restriction. The goal is to make protection inherent to the content itself, not reliant on user behavior.

Labels also support life cycle governance. By tagging information with retention or deletion policies, you ensure that Copilot draws from accurate, current, and purposeful data sources rather than outdated repositories that could surface irrelevant or risky content.

AI-generated content now follows the same retention, deletion, and storage rules as any other file in Microsoft 365. Copilot-created documents, summaries, emails, and agent outputs are stored in the user's OneDrive, SharePoint, or Teams location and inherit the sensitivity label, retention policy, and DLP rules applied to that container. This ensures AI output doesn't create a parallel shadow repository and stays inside your existing information governance boundaries.

Oversharing and Data Residency Controls

Oversharing is one of the most common causes of AI risk. Copilot cannot access data it is not permitted to see, but overly permissive sharing within SharePoint or Teams can quietly expand that boundary.

SharePoint Advanced Management (SAM) helps administrators hide sensitive libraries from Copilot indexing through *Restricted Content Discovery* and restrict link-sharing or download capabilities.

In global organizations, Purview Data Loss Prevention (DLP) and Data Location Dashboards ensure compliance with geographic regulations such as GDPR or HIPAA. For Example, a DLP rule can block Copilot from referencing EU-stored payroll files in a US-based chat.

Monitoring, Attestation, and Continuous Improvement

Once Copilot and agents are live, governance becomes a rhythm of observation, validation, and refinement.

Use **Purview Audit (Premium)** to track who accessed what and when. Visualize usage and anomaly trends in **Power BI**, such as which agents generate the most output or when access spikes occur outside business hours.

Integrate these insights with **Microsoft Sentinel** to correlate AI events with *broader security signals* – for example, sign-ins from risky locations, Defender alerts about data exfiltration attempts, or sudden permission escalations in Entra ID. Seeing these together helps detect whether an AI-driven action coincides with a potential compromise.

Microsoft Purview now includes **Data Security Posture Management** (DSPM) for AI, which acts as your central dashboard for AI-related data risk: it surfaces where Copilot touches sensitive data and highlights oversharing patterns or high-risk sites. DSPM becomes your AI-focused risk view, helping you validate that your data governance policies are working as intended.

Each monitoring cycle should confirm ownership and purpose. Every active agent must have a documented steward and renewal date. **Power Automate** can simplify this by sending quarterly reminders for owners to attest that their agent remains current and compliant. Inactive or unverified agents can be automatically flagged for review or decommissioning.

Continuous improvement closes the loop. Findings from audit and attestation feed directly into policy updates – tightening DLP rules, refining sensitivity labels, or adjusting environment boundaries. When these reviews happen on schedule, governance becomes self-sustaining: a living system that learns from its own data.

Key Takeaways

- **Label with intention:** Purview Information Protection enforces boundaries automatically.

- **Prevent oversharing:** SAM and DLP keep data scoped and regionally compliant.

- **Correlate activity:** Sentinel and Defender signals expose unusual AI or identity behavior.

- **Automate reviews:** Power Automate reminds owners to re-attest and retire inactive agents.

- **Evolve continuously:** Monitoring and feedback make governance adaptive and resilient.

Copilot Studio and Advanced Governance

Up to this point, you and I have been working inside the familiar walls of Microsoft 365. Copilot has been reasoning over data that already lives in your tenant, honoring your existing permissions, labels, and policies. Once you step into Copilot Studio, the world changes. You are no longer just consuming intelligence. You are creating it.

Copilot Studio turns your organization into a builder of agents. Makers and developers can connect to external systems, call APIs, orchestrate workflows, and design copilots that feel like digital coworkers. That power is exactly what makes Copilot Studio exciting. It is also what raises the stakes. A single poorly configured connector, an over-privileged environment, or an unreviewed agent can introduce real risk, even if the maker had the best of intentions.

In this section, I focus on how to keep that power safe, scalable, and accountable. Chapter 8 walks through the essentials of Copilot Studio governance. We will look at how to design your environment strategy, isolate risk, control access, govern connectors, apply ALM, and monitor agents after they go live. The goal is simple. You want makers to feel free to experiment, while you still protect your data, your reputation, and your compliance posture.

Chapter 9 then zooms out to governance at scale. Once agents start proving their value, they grow quickly. Business units want their own copilots. Departments begin automating more processes. Without structure, that growth can turn into duplication, inconsistent quality, and unmanaged risk. You will see how a Three-Zone governance model and a Center of Excellence give you an operating system for AI. Together, they let you keep innovation fast where risk is low, and guardrails firm where risk is high.

Think of this section as the bridge between "we are trying Copilot Studio" and "we run Copilot Studio as a strategic platform." By the time you finish these two chapters, you should have a clear mental model for where agents live, who is allowed to build them, how they move from idea to production, and how you keep hundreds of agents aligned with your policies without slowing the organization down.

CHAPTER 8

Copilot Studio Governance Essentials

Governance does not stop at Microsoft 365. Copilot Studio opens the door for makers and developers to create custom agents that reach beyond traditional boundaries. These agents can connect to external data, call APIs, and automate complex workflows. Without clear guardrails, a well-meaning maker can expose data or deploy logic that behaves unpredictably.

Copilot Studio governance ensures that experimentation remains safe, scalable, and compliant. It builds on your tenant controls but adds deeper oversight for environments, connectors, and agent behavior.

Environment Strategy and Isolation

In Copilot Studio, every agent lives inside a **Power Platform environment** – a logical and secure space where you store, manage, and share your organization's business data, apps, and agents.

Development environments are used for experimentation with sample or anonymized data. Sandbox/Test environments are used to validate agents and collect feedback before release. Production environments host

© Suvidha Shashikumar 2026
S. Shashikumar, *Governance in Microsoft 365 Copilot & Copilot Studio*,
Apress Pocket Guides, https://doi.org/10.1007/979-8-8688-2344-2_8

only approved agents that work with live business data and real users. This separation keeps innovation flexible while protecting operational stability.

Transitions between these stages should follow a structured **Application Lifecycle Management (ALM)** process, using **Power Platform Pipelines**, **Azure DevOps**, or **GitHub Actions** to move solutions safely through Dev ➤ Test ➤ Prod.

Environment-Level Governance Settings

Before creating agents, administrators should configure environment-level AI controls in Power Platform Admin Center (PPAC), such as toggling Generative AI Orchestration and controlling Bing Search integration. Applying these settings consistently across Dev, Test, and Prod environments enforces compliance and prevents unintended exposure of sensitive data.

Knowledge Source Restrictions

You'll want to define which knowledge sources your agents can access. This is where most accidental governance gaps come from. In PPAC, use Data Loss Prevention (DLP) policies to block sensitive sites or libraries in SharePoint and OneDrive. Block public websites and external documents to prevent agents from pulling data from uncontrolled sources.

Publishing Controls

Copilot Studio supports admin-enforced publishing controls that ensure agents cannot bypass your environment strategy. Administrators can require routing through Dev ➤ Test ➤ Prod, restrict makers from publishing directly into production, or mandate approval before an agent can be shared broadly. These controls prevent accidental deployment of untested agents and ensure all solutions follow your zoning and ALM standards.

Maker Onboarding and Compliance Messaging

To reinforce responsible usage, configure maker onboarding experiences in Power Platform Admin Center (PPAC). Use welcome banners and compliance reminders to highlight organizational policies, data handling rules, and security requirements. These messages should appear when makers access environments or create agents, ensuring awareness of governance standards from the start.

A **Managed Environment** is a Power Platform capability that adds an extra layer of governance and insight to any environment. It helps administrators manage growth, monitor activity, and enforce consistent practices across makers. In the **Power Platform Admin Center**, Managed Environments enable you to view usage and sharing analytics at the environment level, limit sharing and enforce solution-based development, gain visibility into capacity, connector usage, DLP compliance, and so on.

When regulatory or contractual requirements demand data residency, create environments in specific geographic regions (e.g., EU or the USA) and restrict agents to connect to data hosted in those same regions.

Each environment should have an assigned owner and life cycle plan. The governance team or Center of Excellence (CoE) should periodically review environment activity to confirm that it still serves an active business purpose. Inactive or redundant environments should be archived or deleted to control cost and complexity.

Use **Power Automate** or **Power Platform Pipelines** to automate review notifications and decommissioning workflows. This keeps the platform lean while maintaining accountability.

Access Control and Role Design

Strong access control keeps governance practical. It defines who can create agents, what data they can use, and how far those agents can reach. In Copilot Studio, permissions are enforced through a combination of Microsoft Entra ID, Power Platform role-based access control (RBAC), and Data Loss Prevention (DLP) policies.

User Identity, Licensing, and Role-Based Access

Identity is where all Copilot Studio governance begins. Every action a maker takes – creating an agent, updating logic, publishing a version, and so on – runs under their Entra ID account. That means the same controls that protect Microsoft 365 apply here automatically. When you enforce MFA, conditional access, or compliant device requirements, you're also protecting how agents are created and used. Nothing changes; the guardrails simply extend into Copilot Studio.

Agents as identities: Microsoft is evolving agents to function as first-class identities in Entra ID, similar to service principals. When this matures, you'll be able to assign permissions directly to agents, track their usage, and even apply life cycle policies to them. In practical terms, this will make least-privilege enforcement far easier because you're no longer guessing what an agent "might" be able to touch – you'll see it clearly.

Licensing: A maker can only build agents if they're licensed to do so. If you assign someone a Copilot Studio authoring license, you're giving them a seat at the table – they can open Copilot Studio, build agents, and publish updates. If they don't have a license, they can still *use* agents, but they can't create or modify them.

You'll want to regularly audit these assignments in the Microsoft 365 Admin Center or Power Platform Admin Center. As people move teams and change their roles, a license that made sense last quarter may not make sense now.

Roles: Administrators should assign roles and permissions deliberately in Power Platform Admin Center, limiting who can create, edit, or publish agents. Some key roles include

- **Environment Admins** manage security, DLP, connector policies, and capacity at the environment level.

- **Makers (Environment Maker)** can create agents, apps, flows, and related assets within an environment.

- **Users** interact with finished agents through approved channels.

External or guest users cannot create or publish agents in Copilot Studio. They can only interact with agents that have been shared with them, provided sharing policies allow it.

Administrators should review guest access settings in Microsoft Entra ID and Power Platform Admin Center, Ensure DLP and environment policies apply consistently to guests and avoid granting elevated roles (such as Environment Maker) to external accounts.

Copilot Studio does not provide a global toggle to disable agent creation. Governance is enforced through Data Loss Prevention (DLP) policies to block risky connectors and data flows, Role-based permissions in Power Platform Admin Center to limit who can create or publish agents and Environment routing and isolation to ensure agents follow Dev ➤ Test ➤ Prod paths.

Data Loss Prevention (DLP) and Connector Governance

Data Loss Prevention (DLP) policies define how data can move across connectors in the Power Platform and Copilot Studio. These policies are the backbone of connector governance, ensuring that copilots and agents never combine data from trusted internal systems with untrusted or public services.

Administrators can configure DLP policies in the Power Platform Admin Center, where connectors are grouped into categories:

- **Business connectors**: Internal and trusted systems such as Dataverse, SharePoint, Outlook, or Teams

- **Non-business connectors:** Public or external services like Twitter, Gmail, or Dropbox

- **Blocked:** Systems or services you want to block completely under any circumstances

Copilot Studio automatically enforces these groupings. For example, if Dataverse connector is in the *Business group* and Dropbox connector is in *Non-business*, a maker cannot build an agent that copies company data to Dropbox.

You should use tenant-level DLP policies for organization-wide rules and environment-level policies for more granular control. Tenant-level policies might restrict all agents from using social media connectors, while environment-level ones can allow specific connectors for approved pilot programs.

For additional precision, you can use connector endpoint filtering to restrict connections to specific domains or API endpoints.

Microsoft now supports scoped connector controls, allowing administrators to restrict connectors to approved domains, APIs, or specific data sources. This gives far more granular governance over what agents can access – preventing unintended data movement even when a connector itself is allowed by DLP.

Review DLP configurations quarterly to align them with evolving data policies and new connectors added by Microsoft or third parties. Out-of-date DLP settings are one of the most common causes of accidental data exposure.

Agent-Level Governance

Once environments, access controls and connector policies are in place, governance must extend to the agents themselves. Every agent built in Copilot Studio is a digital asset that can access data, execute actions, and influence business outcomes. Without oversight, even well-intentioned agents can introduce risk – connecting to unapproved data, exposing sensitive information, or producing inconsistent results.

Ownership and Accountability

Each agent should have a clearly identified owner responsible for its purpose, data connections, and ongoing maintenance. Ownership establishes accountability – it defines who updates the agent, who reviews its performance, and who responds if issues arise.

Document ownership and contact details centrally in a governance registry or dashboard, ideally maintained by the governance lead or CoE.

When an agent owner leaves the organization, reassign ownership immediately to avoid orphaned copilots running unattended.

Governance teams can use Power Automate or Power Platform Pipelines to trigger review workflows when ownership changes or inactivity thresholds are met.

Testing and Quality Assurance is super-important. Testing ensures that agents behave reliably before they reach users. Each new or updated agent should go through a controlled validation process in a test or UAT environment, where reviewers can evaluate accuracy, tone, and compliance with data boundaries.

For example, a customer support copilot trained on product manuals should not produce responses that contradict the official documentation or reveal internal notes.

Testing should verify that

- The agent retrieves only intended data.

- Responses remain accurate and aligned with approved content.

- Sensitive data is not exposed in prompts or outputs.

Automated validation can be integrated into ALM pipelines using Power Platform Pipelines or Azure DevOps, ensuring agents cannot move to production until tests pass.

Agent Monitoring and Behavior Review

Once an agent goes live, governance shifts from configuration to observation. This is where you see how your agents behave in the real world – how they respond to users, what data they touch, and whether they drift from their intended purpose. I've learned that a lot of governance issues don't show up during development; they surface only after users start interacting with an agent at scale.

You'll rely on three main sources for this visibility – **Copilot Studio Analytics, Power Platform Admin Center telemetry, Microsoft Purview audit logs.** Together, they give you a full picture of what the agent is doing, how often it's used, and whether it's staying inside the guardrails you defined earlier.

Governance teams should review this telemetry during operational reviews, looking for sudden spikes in activity or data access, failed conversations or repeated user complaints and high API call volumes or unexpected connector usage.

When monitoring reveals issues, document the corrective action taken such as refining prompts, tightening DLP policies, or retraining the agent with approved data.

This feedback loop ensures agents stay aligned with both user expectations and governance policy.

Change Control and Versioning

Agents aren't static. They evolve as your business evolves – new data sources, improved prompts, updated logic, and refined behaviors. Because of that, you need a clean and predictable way to track every change. Without versioning, even a small update can introduce unintended behavior, and you won't know what changed or how to roll it back.

Use ALM pipelines or source control (Azure DevOps or GitHub) as your single source of truth. When you package agent updates inside solutions, every version becomes traceable. You can see who made changes, when they made them, and what was modified.

Versioning also gives you practical safety. If a new release breaks a workflow, surfaces incorrect information, or violates a data policy, you can instantly roll back to a stable version. It's one of the simplest forms of risk mitigation, and also one of the most effective.

Human Oversight with Agents

Even the best-governed agents require human judgment. Some agents touch sensitive data, trigger high-impact workflows, or generate content that represents your organization. In those moments, you don't want a fully autonomous agent making decisions on its own.

Your governance model should preserve a "human-in-the-loop" step for any agent that carries risk – especially those that automate decisions or send external communications. Human oversight isn't about slowing things down; it's about adding a final layer of review where it actually matters. Sometimes that means approving an action, validating a response, or reviewing outputs before they reach users or customers.

Build this into your governance rhythm. Decide which agents need human approval, define the reviewers, and make sure the process is simple enough that people actually follow it. Human-in-the-loop is how you blend speed with responsibility. It keeps agents aligned with your standards while still delivering the efficiency gains you built them for.

Application Lifecycle Management (ALM) of Agents

Copilot Studio makes it incredibly easy to build agents fast, but speed without structure creates long-term risk. ALM gives you the discipline to move every agent through a consistent path: designed, tested, approved, deployed, and reviewed. When you treat agents like any other enterprise solution, you protect yourself from accidental breakage and unintentional behavior.

ALM provides the framework that carries an agent safely from idea to production. It ensures that every version is tested, approved, and traceable, and that nothing reaches users without passing through the right checks.

ALM Tools and Pipelines

Copilot Studio agents are packaged and moved using Power Platform solutions, so they can move through the same ALM tools that support Power Apps applications and Power Automate flows.

Common options include

- **Power Platform Pipelines:** The simplest way to automate deployment between Development, Test, and Production environments directly within the Power Platform Admin Center

- **Azure DevOps Pipelines:** For organizations that need custom automation, validation, or integration with broader DevOps workflows

- **GitHub Actions:** Lightweight automation for source control and deployment in cloud-native teams

All these tools support consistent packaging, testing, and deployment while maintaining change history and governance sign-offs.

Versioning, Testing, and Approval Gates

Every agent version should go through controlled stages before anyone uses it. Power Platform Pipelines usually define these as deployment stages with manual or automated approval gates. Approvers, often governance leads or environment admins, verify that DLP policies are correct, testing has passed in a non-production environment, and the agent's ownership, metadata, and documentation are complete.

You can also embed automated compliance checks here so that an agent is validated against security and data policies before deployment.

Once the approver signs off, the pipeline promotes the agent to the next stage. This gives you a clean digital paper trail and ensures that only validated agents ever reach production.

Versioning inside Power Platform Pipelines, Azure DevOps, or GitHub also allows you to restore previous builds quickly. If a new release introduces performance issues, compliance problems, or breaks something important, rollback becomes a simple and safe option. This remains one of the most effective ways to reduce operational risk in agent governance.

Monitoring and Analytics

Once agents are live, visibility must extend beyond data protection to how each agent behaves, performs, and evolves. This form of monitoring focuses on usage, performance, quality, and accountability – ensuring copilots continue to operate responsibly long after deployment.

Built-In Copilot Studio Analytics

Copilot Studio includes native analytics that provide insights into how agents are used in real scenarios. Agent owners and Administrators can view metrics such as conversation volume, active users, satisfaction scores, and topic engagement. These reports reveal how well an agent serves its intended purpose.

For example, if a helpdesk agent handles most inquiries but triggers frequent escalation, analytics can point to knowledge gaps that need retraining or redesign.

This type of monitoring differs from tenant-level oversight because it measures agent effectiveness, not data access.

Telemetry via Power Platform Admin Center and Purview Audit

The Power Platform Admin Center provides operational telemetry at the environment level, showing which agents are most active, which connectors they use, and how makers are updating them.

Microsoft Purview Audit extends this traceability to individual interactions, recording when agents are accessed, what data they reference, and whether any exceptions occur.

Together, these insights allow governance teams to connect agent behavior to policy enforcement.

For instance, if a marketing agent begins using connectors outside approved policies, Purview audit logs will surface that deviation for immediate review.

Visualization and Reporting with Power BI

Power BI can consolidate Copilot Studio analytics, audit data, and environment telemetry into unified dashboards that focus on agent performance and impact.

These dashboards can show which agents deliver measurable business outcomes, which are underused, and where optimization opportunities exist.

For example, a dashboard may highlight that 70% of support queries are now resolved by agents, providing a tangible measure of ROI and reliability.

Unlike enterprise compliance reporting, this level of analytics helps teams evaluate how well agents serve people and processes, not just whether they stay compliant.

Integration with Microsoft Sentinel for Security Signals

When agents operate at enterprise scale, integrating their telemetry with Microsoft Sentinel provides security-context awareness. Sentinel can correlate agent activity with broader signals such as identity risk, data movement, or unusual login patterns. This allows security teams to detect misuse or compromised connectors early. For example, a sudden increase in API calls or off-hours activity may indicate misconfiguration or automation loops that require intervention.

Continuous Feedback and Governance Improvement

Monitoring is most valuable when it drives action. The insights collected from Copilot Studio analytics, audit logs, and Power BI dashboards should feed directly into your governance rhythm – helping teams refine rules, retrain copilots, and evolve policies based on real usage. Governance councils or Center of Excellence (CoE) teams can use this feedback to identify what works and what needs adjustment.

For example, telemetry showing low engagement might prompt simplification of prompts or consolidation of redundant agents, while consistently high usage may justify scaling an agent to new departments.

This continuous improvement loop transforms governance from a static compliance exercise into an adaptive system that learns alongside your organization.

Measuring What Matters: Governance Metrics and Reporting

Monitoring provides visibility, but governance requires measurable outcomes. Define clear KPIs and reporting mechanisms to track compliance, operational performance, and adoption. These metrics turn raw telemetry into actionable insights for leadership and governance councils, reinforcing the Responsible AI principles of reliability and accountability by ensuring agents remain trustworthy and aligned with organizational standards.

Compliance indicators demonstrate whether agents adhere to organizational policies and regulatory requirements. Examples include the percentage of agents reviewed within a governance cycle, the number of policy violations detected and resolved, and audit readiness scores based on Purview checks. These measures confirm that governance is not just theoretical but actively enforced.

Operational performance metrics focus on resilience and reliability. Tracking agent uptime and availability against disaster recovery objectives, monitoring mean time to recovery during incidents, and analyzing the frequency and resolution of alerts provide insight into how well the system responds under stress. These measures ensure that governance supports continuity and user trust.

Adoption and value metrics reveal whether agents deliver meaningful impact. Conversation volume, user satisfaction scores, and ratios of active to inactive agents highlight engagement. ROI indicators, such as the percentage of support queries resolved by agents, connect governance to tangible business outcomes.

Reporting should consolidate these insights into accessible formats. Power BI dashboards can unify Copilot Studio analytics, Purview audit logs, and environment telemetry into a single view. Governance scorecards provide leadership with a concise summary during monthly or quarterly reviews, while automated alerts in Power Platform Admin Center and Microsoft Sentinel ensure real-time visibility into compliance and risk signals.

Finally, governance should operate on a predictable rhythm. Monthly operational reviews, quarterly compliance audits, and annual maturity assessments create a cycle of continuous improvement. This cadence transforms governance from a static checklist into a dynamic system that evolves with organizational needs.

By combining monitoring with measurable outcomes, governance shifts from passive oversight to active accountability – ensuring agents remain reliable, secure, and aligned with organizational goals.

Disaster Recovery and Availability

Business continuity is critical for Copilot Studio agents. Governance must ensure that services remain available during outages and can recover quickly without data loss or compliance breaches.

- **Failover Strategy:** Implement geo-redundancy and backup environments for critical workloads. Use Azure Site Recovery or equivalent for high availability.

- **Recovery Objectives:** Define Recovery Time Objective (RTO) and Recovery Point Objective (RPO) for agent restoration and data recovery.

- **Backup and Restore Procedures:** Document steps for restoring agent configurations, connectors, and ALM versions. Include automated rollback capabilities in pipelines.

- **Testing and Validation:** Conduct periodic DR drills and maintain audit logs of results. Update plans based on lessons learned.

- **Monitoring and Alerts:** Integrate telemetry and anomaly detection with Microsoft Sentinel. Configure automated alerts for downtime events and recovery progress.

- **Compliance:** Ensure DR plans meet regulatory requirements (GDPR, HIPAA) and maintain audit readiness.

- **Roles and Responsibilities:** Define escalation paths and RACI mapping for DR activities to ensure accountability during incidents.

Cost Controls and Consumption Management

Managing cost is a critical part of governance for Copilot Studio. While administrators often ask about hard spend limits, Copilot Studio does not support maximum spend caps. Instead, governance relies on proactive monitoring and alerts.

- **Consumption Alerts**: Configure alerts for prepaid message packs and pay-as-you-go billing thresholds in Power Platform Admin Center and Azure Cost Management.

- **Usage Reporting**: Review usage analytics regularly to identify spikes in consumption.

- **License Reviews**: Audit license assignments to prevent uncontrolled growth.

- **Budget Forecasting**: Use historical consumption data to predict future costs and allocate budgets accordingly.

Important Note   There is no feature to enforce hard spend limits. Administrators must rely on alerts and monitoring to manage costs effectively.

Beyond monitoring and forecasting, organizations should define how Copilot Studio costs are allocated internally. Use Power Platform Admin Center analytics and Azure Cost Management reports to track consumption by environment or department. Implement internal chargeback or showback models to distribute costs fairly and encourage responsible usage. This approach promotes transparency and helps business units plan budgets effectively.

Community and Training Strategy

Governance is only effective when makers and stakeholders understand and embrace it. Establish a structured adoption plan that includes role-based training for makers, admins, and business users. Go beyond formal training by creating a vibrant community:

- Organize internal showcases, hackathons, and champion programs to promote best practices and innovation within guardrails.

- Use dedicated channels (Teams, Yammer, or internal portals) to share updates, compliance tips, and success stories.

- Encourage peer learning and recognition to build a culture of responsible AI development.

A strong community and training strategy ensures makers feel supported, compliance becomes second nature, and innovation thrives without compromising governance.

Key Takeaways

- Every agent is a governed digital asset that must operate within defined environments and access boundaries.

- A clear environment strategy supported by ALM pipelines and Managed Environments, keeps experimentation and production safely separated.

- Licensing and role assignments work together to define who can create, manage, and use agents; both must align for secure governance.

- Data Loss Prevention (DLP) policies and connector governance prevent sensitive information from crossing trust boundaries.

- Ownership and accountability ensure each agent has a responsible steward throughout its life cycle.

- Versioning, approval gates, and rollback plans bring discipline and traceability to every update.

- Agent-level monitoring focuses on performance, adoption, and compliance, transforming analytics into actionable governance insights.

- Continuous feedback turns governance into a living system that evolves with real usage and organizational maturity.

CHAPTER 9

Scaling Governance – Zoned Model and Center of Excellence

As your agents start proving their value, adoption accelerates fast. Teams start building their own agents, departments ask for AI automation, and use cases pop up everywhere. I've seen this pattern in every organization that crosses the first threshold of AI maturity.

But here's the reality:

If you don't set up structure early, adoption grows in ways that create duplication, inconsistent quality, and unmanaged risk.

Scaling governance is how you let innovation stay fast **without** creating chaos. At scale, governance stops being "policies and controls" and becomes an operating model – something people follow instinctively because it makes work easier, not harder.

Two frameworks help you get there:

- **The Three-Zone Governance Model**: Keeps experimentation and production from stepping on each other

- **The Center of Excellence (CoE)**: The engine that makes governance real across people, processes, and platforms

S. Shashikumar, *Governance in Microsoft 365 Copilot & Copilot Studio*,
Apress Pocket Guides, https://doi.org/10.1007/979-8-8688-2344-2_9

Together, they give you a system that lets hundreds of agents thrive safely, efficiently, and in alignment with your strategy.

The Three Governance Zones

The Three-Zone Governance Model classifies agents and environments based on risk, data sensitivity, and maturity. Each zone applies a level of control proportionate to its purpose – ensuring that experimentation and production can coexist without conflict.

Innovation Zone: This is a safe space where makers and developers can explore ideas and build prototypes without worrying about breaking anything. Guardrails such as Data Loss Prevention (DLP) policies and connector restrictions prevent access to sensitive data, while optional Managed Environments provide visibility and monitoring to avoid sprawl. The goal is to enable rapid learning and innovation while minimizing organizational risk.

Controlled Zone: Here's where an idea starts becoming a reliable business tool. Governance becomes more structured with approvals for new connectors and environment changes, and Application Lifecycle Management (ALM) pipelines enforce solution movement across development, test, and production environments. Documentation, metadata, and clear ownership are required for every solution, giving teams confidence in reliability without sacrificing agility.

Restricted Zone: This zone handles your high-sensitivity or regulated workloads like finance, HR, legal, healthcare, or anything that requires strict oversight. Only approved makers can build here. Compliance is maintained through continuous audit logging with Microsoft Purview and advanced monitoring with Microsoft Sentinel. Strict DLP policies, conditional access, and versioning for every change ensures end-to-end security and compliance.

Admin-enforced publishing approvals ensure only reviewed and compliant agents make their way into the Controlled or Restricted zones. This zoning model keeps governance adaptive with fast innovation in low-risk spaces and strong protection where sensitive data lives.

Implementing Zoning in Microsoft 365 and Copilot Studio

Zoning becomes real through environment configuration and layered policy across Microsoft 365 and Copilot Studio. Each zone maps to a set of Power Platform environments with their own controls and visibility.

For example:

- **Innovation Zone:** Sandbox environments with limited connectors, no access to production data, and monitoring for sprawl

- **Controlled Zone:** Managed environments integrated with ALM pipelines, structured approvals, and solution life cycle enforcement

- **Restricted Zone**: Production environments with strict connector policies, audit logging, conditional access, and integration with Microsoft Sentinel for advanced threat monitoring

Tenant administrators can manage zoning through the Power Platform Admin Center by defining who can build in each environment, what data sources are available, and how agents are promoted between zones. The governance council or CoE should maintain a promotion framework – a documented path that defines when and how an agent graduates from one zone to another.

Zoning works best when supported by Managed Environments and Data Loss Prevention (DLP) policies. These tools enforce the boundaries defined by each zone and provide telemetry to ensure compliance remains transparent.

The Center of Excellence (CoE) Model

The Center of Excellence (CoE) is the human engine behind governance at scale.

It combines policy, enablement, and analytics into a unified practice that drives both control and innovation.

A well-run CoE serves as both an enabler and a guardian – supporting maker innovation while ensuring enterprise standards are upheld.

Key functions of a mature CoE include

- **Governance Operations:** Manage environment provisioning, DLP policy updates, and license distribution.

- **Enablement and Training:** Provide documentation, templates, and best practices to help makers build responsibly.

- **Monitoring and Reporting:** Aggregate analytics from Copilot Studio, Power BI, and Purview to track usage, compliance, and adoption.

- **Innovation Acceleration:** Identify high-value agents and help departments scale them organization-wide.

- **Continuous Improvement:** Feed lessons from analytics and audits back into governance strategy.

Microsoft's Power Platform CoE Starter Kit offers a strong starting point, with automation and dashboards that can be extended for Copilot Studio governance. Over time, most organizations evolve from one central CoE into a federated model, where departmental CoEs manage their own environments under the standards set by the central governance body.

Why RACI Strengthens AI Governance

As you scale your use of AI agents, governance naturally becomes more complex. CIOs, CoE leads, IT admins, security teams, and business stakeholders all play a role in keeping agents safe and useful. A simple RACI model, which identifies who is Responsible, Accountable, Consulted, and Informed, brings clarity to this shared ecosystem. It reduces ambiguity, prevents overlap, and ensures that every governance activity has a clear owner.

RACI fits naturally with zoned governance because each zone has different expectations and degrees of oversight. The CoE usually serves as the governance hub, owning standards, templates, and training across all zones. IT stays responsible for platform safety, environment configuration, and connector governance. Security and compliance teams provide guidance when agents touch regulated or sensitive data. Business units stay informed through training and maker guidance, while remaining accountable for the correctness and outcomes of the agents they create.

In practice, many organizations use RACI to track ownership as the CoE matures:

- **Responsible**: The CoE Lead creating governance standards

- **Accountable**: The CIO ensuring alignment with enterprise strategy

- **Consulted**: Security and compliance teams providing risk and regulatory input

- **Informed**: Makers and business units who need awareness and guardrails

RACI strengthens governance in three ways. It brings clarity to ownership, preventing the friction that shows up when tasks fall between teams. It creates a consistent structure that scales as organizations move from pilots to full production. And it reinforces compliance by making accountability visible. When each role is defined clearly, agents become safer and innovation becomes faster and more predictable.

Key Takeaways

- **Governance must scale with adoption.**

  As agents spread across teams and departments, the risk surface grows. A scalable governance model ensures innovation doesn't outpace safety.

- **The Three-Zone Model keeps innovation fast and production safe.**

  Innovation, Controlled, and Restricted zones create clear boundaries for what can be built, where, and under what guardrails. Low-risk experimentation stays flexible; high-risk workloads stay tightly governed.

- **Environment zoning is the backbone of Copilot Studio governance.**

  Each zone maps to a dedicated Power Platform environment with its own connector policies, ALM rules, approvals, and DLP boundaries – keeping environments purpose-built and predictable.

- **The Center of Excellence is both an engine and a safety net.**

  A mature CoE operationalizes governance through standards, templates, analytics, training, and environment strategy while accelerating high-value use cases across the organization.

- **RACI reduces confusion as multiple teams begin participating.**

  Clear ownership (Responsible, Accountable, Consulted, Informed) prevents overlap, eliminates bottlenecks, and ensures every governance activity – from labeling to life cycle to approvals – has a clear steward.

- **Governance becomes an operating model, not a checklist.**

  When zoning, CoE functions and RACI work together, governance shifts from reactive policing to a proactive system that supports growth, safety, and continuous improvement.

- **Adaptive governance = sustainable scale.**

  The right mix of environment separation, policy layering, ownership clarity, and analytics ensures agents can grow from a handful to hundreds without losing compliance, consistency, or trust.

Reference and Future Outlook

Governance becomes real when it moves beyond concepts into daily practice. This section brings together everything you need to operationalize Copilot and agent governance at scale – clear checklists, repeatable patterns, audit-ready evidence, and a maturity roadmap that shows how your organization evolves over time.

Earlier sections explained the principles, controls, and life cycle patterns behind responsible AI. Section 4 shifts the focus from *why* to *how*: how to verify your configuration, how to prepare for audits, how to monitor agents after deployment, and how to guide your organization from early guardrails to predictive, adaptive oversight.

This is the part of the book you'll return to most often. It provides a complete governance reference toolkit and pairs it with a forward-looking outlook on where AI governance is heading – more autonomous agents, richer telemetry, deeper collaboration between IT and business teams, and a growing emphasis on continuous visibility rather than periodic checks.

If the earlier chapters helped you design the framework, this section helps you **run it** – consistently, confidently, and with clarity about what comes next.

CHAPTER 10

Governance Reference Toolkit

Governance only becomes sustainable when it is *repeatable*. After working with dozens of enterprises, I've learned that the difference between organizations that manage AI confidently and those that struggle is rarely technical – it's operational. Teams need clarity on *what to configure, where to configure it, how it should be implemented, and when each control applies*. Without that structure, even the best governance strategy falls apart as usage grows.

This chapter turns governance from theory into an actionable system. This is your complete, end-to-end reference toolkit: tenant controls, data boundaries, connector rules, deployment steps, monitoring signals, audit evidence, and life cycle checks – all mapped directly to the Copilot Control System (CCS). Every table and checklist in this chapter is meant to be used, not just read. Whether you're preparing for a go-live, validating compliance, or responding to a security review, this chapter gives you the exact levers and locations you need.

© Suvidha Shashikumar 2026
S. Shashikumar, *Governance in Microsoft 365 Copilot & Copilot Studio*,
Apress Pocket Guides, https://doi.org/10.1007/979-8-8688-2344-2_10

Tenant-Level Controls

Tenant-level controls create the security and compliance foundation for both **Microsoft 365 Copilot** and **Copilot Studio Agents**. These tenant controls map directly to the "Security and Governance" and "Management Controls" pillars of the Copilot Control System (CCS).

Table 10-1 covers the core identity controls – MFA, Conditional Access, admin privilege management, and who can use Copilot Studio Lite. Explains where each setting lives and when it applies.

Table 10-1. *Identity and Access*

	What	Where (tools)	How	Applies to
✓	Enforce MFA and Conditional Access	Entra ID ➤ Conditional Access	Require MFA, compliant device, session restrictions	Both
✓	Role reviews and least-privilege admin access	Entra ID ➤ Roles & Administrators	Remove unused admin roles; apply PIM	Both
✓	Block legacy authentication	Entra ID ➤ Authentication Methods	Disable legacy protocols	Both
✓	Control who can use Copilot Studio Lite (Agent Builder)	M365 Admin Center ➤ Integrated Apps/ Settings	Enable per security group or disable tenant-wide	M365 Copilot

Table 10-2 defines how sensitivity labels, data residency rules, and content restrictions shape what Copilot and agents can access. Includes how labels propagate and how to hide sites from Copilot.

Table 10-2. *Data Boundaries and Sensitivity Labels*

	What	Where (tools)	How	Applies to
✅	Apply sensitivity labels across all content	Purview ➤ Information Protection	Label SharePoint, Teams, OneDrive, Outlook content	Both
✅	Hide sensitive sites from Copilot	SharePoint Admin ➤ SAM ➤ Restricted Content Discovery	Disable Copilot indexing per site	M365 Copilot
✅	Enforce regional/geo data boundaries	Purview ➤ Data Location Dashboard	Restrict EU/regulated data	Both
✅	Ensure AI-generated files inherit labels and retention	OneDrive/SharePoint + Purview Retention Policies	AI output stored in governed locations automatically inherits labels and life cycle rules	Both

Table 10-3 outlines how DLP rules restrict Copilot and agent access to sensitive content, prevent oversharing, and control connector endpoints for safer AI actions.

Table 10-3. *DLP and Data Protection Policies*

	What	Where (tools)	How	Applies to
✓	Protect credentials, PII, financial data	Purview ➤ DLP Policies	Block or warn on files containing sensitive data before Copilot consumes it	Both
✓	Restrict Copilot/ agents from accessing Highly Confidential files	Purview DLP + Sensitivity Labels	Create DLP rule "Block agent access to HC content"	Both
✓	Monitor oversharing	Purview ➤ Data Risk Hub	Weekly oversharing assessment for sites grounded in agents	Both
✓	Restrict connector endpoints	Power Platform Admin Center ➤ DLP Policies	Use endpoint filtering to allow only approved domains/APIs	Copilot Studio Agents

Table 10-4 shows how to manage allowed/banned connectors, review agent/app permissions, and enforce plugin rules to reduce risk across Microsoft 365 and Copilot Studio.

Table 10-4. *Connector and App Controls*

	What	Where (tools)	How	Applies to
✔	Manage allowed/banned connectors	Power Platform Admin Center ➤ DLP Policies	Group connectors as Business/Non-Business/ Blocked	Copilot Studio Agents
✔	Approve/block agents/apps	M365 Admin Center ➤ Integrated Apps	Review metadata, permissions, publisher attestation	Both
✔	Enforce plugin usage rules	M365 Admin Center ➤ Copilot Control System	Approve external plugins; restrict high-risk ones	M365 Copilot

Table 10-5 summarizes the logging and monitoring capabilities needed to track AI behavior, identify anomalies, and respond quickly to risky activity.

Table 10-5. *Logging and Monitoring*

	What	Where (tools)	How	Applies to
✔	Enable Copilot logging	Purview Audit (Standard/Premium)	Capture prompts, responses, and actions	Both
✔	Monitor anomalies	Microsoft Sentinel + Defender XDR	Correlate AI activity with identity events	Both
✔	Track DLP, SAM, and sharing alerts	Purview Alerts	Set automatic notifications for risky behaviors	Both

Deployment and Monitoring Checklists

A deployment checklist ensures every agent or Copilot experience enters the environment deliberately, not by accident. The Copilot Control System (CCS) defines what organizations should measure – usage, adoption, readiness, and risk. Reporting is surfaced through existing admin centers: Copilot analytics in the Microsoft 365 Admin Center, agent analytics in the Power Platform Admin Center, and risk insights through Purview and Sentinel. Reviewing these signals regularly ensures governance decisions are grounded in real usage patterns.

Table 10-6 provides a concise, end-to-end list of everything that must be validated before an agent or Copilot experience goes live – ownership, purpose, data grounding, connector approvals, ALM checks, access reviews, and monitoring readiness.

Table 10-6. *Deployment Checklist (Before Go-Live)*

	What	Where (tools)	How	Applies to
✔	Ownership defined	Solution Document/ CoE Intake	Assign business owner + technical steward	Both
✔	Purpose and scope documented	CoE Intake/Dev environment	Clear problem statement, value, and risks	Both
✔	Grounding data reviewed	SharePoint/ Dataverse/SAM	Remove risky/ unnecessary data	Both
✔	Data masking applied	Purview ➤ Data Masking Rules	Mask personal/ sensitive fields	Copilot Studio Agents
✔	Connector approvals complete	PPAC ➤ DLP	Verify connectors allowed in environment	Copilot Studio Agents

(continued)

Table 10-6. (*continued*)

	What	Where (tools)	How	Applies to
✓	Agents tested in Dev/Sandbox	Copilot Studio ➤ Test Environment	Conversation tests + functional validation	Copilot Studio Agents
✓	ALM pipeline approval	Power Platform Pipelines/ADO/GH Actions	Approver verifies DLP, data, and versioning	Copilot Studio Agents
✓	Access control reviewed	PPAC/Entra	Confirm only necessary roles can publish	Copilot Studio Agents
✓	Plugin and extension approval	M365 Admin ➤ Integrated Apps	Validate permissions and publisher attestation	M365 Copilot
✓	Monitoring enabled	Purview + PPAC	Audit logs, telemetry, alerts active	Both

Table 10-7 provides a clear set of ongoing checks to ensure safe and effective operations post-deployment – usage trends, performance signals, access anomalies, oversharing risks, ownership attestation, and cost monitoring.

Table 10-7. *Monitoring Checklist (After Go-Live)*

	What	Where (tools)	How	Applies to
✓	Conversation volume and performance	Copilot Studio Analytics	Identify drop-offs, errors, escalations	Copilot Studio Agents
✓	Usage and adoption trends	M365 Admin ➤ Copilot Reports	Track who is using, how often, and for what	M365 Copilot
✓	Data access anomalies	Purview ➤ Audit	Look for unusual access, spikes, or label violations	Both
✓	Identity anomalies	Sentinel/ Defender	Correlate AI events with sign-ins or risk events	Both
✓	Oversharing or risky content exposure	Purview ➤ Data Risk	Weekly oversharing assessments	Copilot Studio Agents
✓	Ownership attestation	Power Automate workflow	Quarterly "Does this agent still need to exist?"	Copilot Studio Agents
✓	Cost consumption	PPAC ➤ Billing/ Cost Estimator	Track messaging usage, overages, trends	Copilot Studio Agents

Audit and Compliance Readiness

AI governance isn't complete unless you can prove it. This section gives you the essential evidence paths needed during security reviews, internal audits, or regulatory checks – so you can respond quickly, confidently, and with complete traceability across both Microsoft 365 Copilot and Copilot Studio agents.

Table 10-8 provides a quick-reference guide showing the evidence required during audits or security reviews – what to provide, where to retrieve it, and which Copilot scenarios it applies to.

Table 10-8. *Audit and Compliance Readiness*

Audit Area	Evidence needed	Where to pull it	Applies to
Identity controls	MFA, CA policies, device compliance	Entra ID	Both
Data protection	Labeling rules, DLP policy configurations	Purview	Both
Content access	Who accessed what, when	Purview Audit	Both
Agent approvals	Pipeline approvals, version logs	PPAC Pipelines/ADO/GitHub	Copilot Studio Agents
Plugin/connector approvals	Integrated Apps metadata	M365 Admin ➤ Integrated Apps	Both
Attestation history	Ownership and renewal history	CoE docs/Automations	Copilot Studio Agents
Life cycle documentation	Purpose, change logs, versions	PPAC Pipelines/ADO/GitHub	Copilot Studio Agents
AI data exposure	Sensitive data touched by Copilot, oversharing patterns, high-risk sites	Purview DSPM for AI	Both

How to Stay Audit-Ready All Year

Automate quarterly attestation workflows to confirm compliance with organizational policies. Enforce versioning and maintain detailed change logs for every agent update. Keep a central Agent Registry in Dataverse or a SharePoint list to track ownership, environment, and life cycle status. Use a Center of Excellence dashboard to monitor flagged content, restricted data usage, DLP violations, anomalous activity, and agent counts by zone (Innovation, Controlled, Restricted). These practices ensure continuous visibility and make regulatory or internal audits faster and less disruptive.

AI Incident Response

Even well-designed agents can behave unexpectedly. When that happens, the goal is to pause, investigate, and correct without disrupting the business. Temporarily unpublish or disable the agent through Copilot Studio or the Microsoft 365 Admin Center. Review evidence through Purview Audit, Copilot logs, and Sentinel alerts to understand what occurred, who was affected, and whether data boundaries were crossed.

Integrate Microsoft Sentinel and Microsoft Defender for proactive threat detection and anomaly monitoring. Configure alerts for suspicious agent activity, unauthorized data access, or policy violations to ensure rapid response.

Once the issue is clear, update the agent's logic or grounding data and redeploy with proper validation. A simple approach works best: pause fast, investigate with facts, correct the design, and restore service.

Governance Maturity Model

As AI capabilities expand, governance cannot remain static. Organizations evolve through recognizable stages – moving from essential guardrails to fully intelligent, adaptive governance. This maturity model helps you understand where your organization stands today and what investments will elevate your readiness as your Copilot and agent footprint grows.

Rather than a checklist, think of this as a **progression**: each level builds on the last, strengthening structure, visibility, and operational discipline.

Level 1: Foundation (Initial)

Early governance with minimal structure.

Characteristics

- No formal Center of Excellence (CoE)

- Agents created ad hoc by teams

- Basic sensitivity labels applied inconsistently

- Little or no usage monitoring or telemetry

What to build next

Establish tenant-level controls, baseline DLP, core sensitivity labeling, and the first set of admin guardrails.

Level 2: Structured (Growing)

Governance practices begin to take shape and expand.

Characteristics

- Central IT owns configuration and key policies

- DLP policies consistently enforced

- Early ALM pipelines appear for agent moves

- Basic analytics dashboards for Copilot and agents

What to build next

Define a formal environment strategy, establish a CoE, create standardized templates, and introduce publishing and intake rules.

Level 3: Scaled (Operationalized)

Governance becomes systematic, predictable, and repeatable.

Characteristics

- Full environment zoning (Innovation ➤ Controlled ➤ Restricted).

- CoE manages training, standards, and review processes.

- Automated owner attestation and quarterly inventory reviews.

- Sentinel + Purview integrated for active security oversight.

What to build next

Optimize governance workflows, measure business value, and adopt continuous monitoring and richer telemetry across environments.

Level 4: Optimized (Adaptive and Predictive)

Governance becomes intelligent, data-driven, and partially self-adjusting.

Characteristics

- Federated CoE: Central standards with distributed ownership

- Real-time anomaly detection linked to identity signals

- Predictive risk scoring for agents and data flows

- Continuous improvement cycles guided by insights

What to build next

Adopt autonomous governance patterns, evolve oversight to proactive risk anticipation, and prepare for next-generation agent behaviors.

What's Next: Agent 365 and Unified Governance

Agent 365 (currently in preview) will expand this maturity model by providing a unified catalog for agent discovery, approval, life cycle tracking, and compliance review – all inside the Microsoft 365 Admin Center. As it matures, it will help consolidate oversight of agents built across SharePoint, Copilot Studio, and pro-code solutions, accelerating organizations toward higher levels of governance maturity.

CHAPTER 11

The Future of AI Governance and How to Begin

As organizations move from experimenting with AI to relying on it as a true digital teammate, governance must evolve alongside capability. What begins as guardrails quickly becomes an ecosystem – a shared commitment across IT, security, operations, and business teams to guide AI behavior intentionally.

As you begin implementing everything in this guide, the most reliable anchor is **the Copilot Control System (CCS)**. CCS is Microsoft's unified governance framework for Copilot – bringing together security and governance, management controls, and measurement and reporting into one model.

Even as Copilot evolves with new agent types, admin controls, and platform capabilities – CCS remains the stable blueprint that ties all your governance decisions together. Treat it as your north star: a simple, durable structure that clarifies *how* every setting, policy, and checklist in this book fits into the bigger picture.

© Suvidha Shashikumar 2026

S. Shashikumar, *Governance in Microsoft 365 Copilot & Copilot Studio*, Apress Pocket Guides, https://doi.org/10.1007/979-8-8688-2344-2_11

In this chapter, we'll look ahead and explore how governance will shift as AI becomes more autonomous, more embedded, and more distributed – and ends with a practical, grounded roadmap your organization can follow immediately.

From Control to Collaboration

Early governance is almost always control-heavy – I've seen this pattern in every major tech wave. Leaders worry about data exposure, misuse, compliance gaps, and the unknown, which is normal. Every major technology wave – cloud, mobile, Low-code transformation – began with IT putting guardrails up before opening doors.

But sustainable AI governance can't stay in that mode – not if you want scale. As maturity grows, governance shifts from *"restrict and protect"* to *"partner and enable."*

Here's what that evolution looks like and how organizations can intentionally move toward it:

1. **From approvals to shared standards**

   Instead of reviewing every new agent manually, you define the **standards** – when teams follow these standards around naming, documentation, testing, and data boundaries, they can build responsibly without waiting for someone to check their work. Standards become the foundation that replaces approval bottlenecks.

2. **From reactive oversight to proactive nudges**

   When organizations rely only on human review, they tend to react to incidents rather than anticipate them. As analytics mature, that reactive model gives

way to early detection. As telemetry improves –
usage spikes, unusual access, odd connector
activity – Copilot Studio, Purview, and Sentinel
start surfacing issues before humans do. Instead of
chasing problems, the system starts nudging owners
and surfacing concerns in advance.

3. **From centralized control to federated collaboration**

A deeper shift happens in ownership. In the
beginning, IT remains at the center of every step.
But as departments gain experience and confidence,
expertise spreads. HR begins building agents for
recruiting. Finance builds agents for reporting.
Operations builds agents for process automation.
Governance naturally becomes a shared model. A
central Center of Excellence (CoE) sets the practices
and policies. Individual departments operate within
those boundaries and knowledge flows in both
directions.

4. **From "IT vs. Business" to shared accountability**

The most profound transformation is cultural.
AI stops feeling like an isolated technology and
becomes an organizational capability. Everyone
shares responsibility. The business owns
correctness, relevance, and outcomes. IT owns
safety, compliance, and platform health. Leadership
ensures that AI supports the broader strategy. When
this balance takes hold, governance turns into a
shared rhythm rather than a set of rules.

This evolution mirrors what happened with cloud adoption and low-code transformation – the pattern is identical, just happening faster this time. When governance shifts from gatekeeping to partnership, innovation increases without increasing risk. Teams build more confidently. Oversight becomes smarter. And AI becomes a capability the entire organization can trust.

The Governance Operating Model for an AI-Driven Organization

As organizations move deeper into AI adoption, I've seen the hardest part isn't configuring controls – it's creating a governance model that actually scales. AI governance can't live in a single team or a single document. It must become a shared operating model that aligns people, processes, and platforms around consistent, predictable, responsible AI behavior.

This section outlines the core elements of that operating model.

1. **Clear Roles and Ownership**

    AI governance becomes real when every agent has clearly defined owners:

    - **Business Owner**: Responsible for purpose and outcomes

    - **Technical Owner**: Responsible for configuration, data sources, and maintenance

    - **Governance Owner**: Responsible for policy alignment and compliance

    I've seen agents fail or drift the moment these roles aren't explicit – ambiguity is the fastest path to unmanaged risk.

2. **A Layered Policy Architecture**

In my experience, a single giant policy always collapses under its own weight. A layered model scales because each layer does one job well. Here's how I break down the layers when helping teams operationalize governance:

- **Tenant-wide controls**: Identity, security, DLP, sensitivity labels

- **Environment controls**: Connector boundaries, data zones, ALM

- **Agent-level controls**: Allowed actions, grounding data, publishing rules

This layering ensures that policies scale with the organization and remain consistent across teams.

3. **Standardized Agent Life Cycle**

Just like applications or APIs, agents mature through stages:

1. **Design** (purpose, data boundaries, allowed actions)

2. **Build** (within approved environments and connectors)

3. **Validate** (testing, access reviews, safety checks)

4. **Deploy** (with monitoring enabled)

5. **Operate** (usage, anomalies, drift tracking)

6. **Review or Retire**

A shared life cycle prevents quiet sprawl. I've seen small "experiment" agents suddenly become mission-critical without monitoring, ownership, or safety checks. Having a standardized life cycle stops that from happening.

4. **Integrated Monitoring and Insights**

Governance only works when it's visible. Without unified telemetry, you're governing in the dark. Your model should unify telemetry from

- Copilot Studio

- Microsoft Purview

- Sentinel

- SharePoint Advanced Management

- Graph Data Connect

This gives you a single view of agent behavior, risk, and usage – so governance becomes proactive instead of reactive.

5. **A Culture of Responsible AI**

Tools and policies can set boundaries, but only culture sustains them.

A mature AI governance model:

- Encourages teams to escalate concerns

- Teaches makers how to design responsibly

- Sets expectations for data handling

- Rewards thoughtful, intentional automation

Culture is the multiplier. I've learned that policies set the boundaries, but culture is what makes people follow them even when nobody's watching.

From Strategy to Action: Operationalizing AI Governance

You don't need perfect governance on day one – none of us ever do. What you need is direction, momentum, and a clear starting point.

1. **Build Governance into the Flow of Work, Not Around It**

   In my experience, governance only succeeds when it becomes part of the natural workflow, not an extra set of steps employees must remember. Instead of adding new approval layers or creating separate compliance portals, the goal is to embed governance directly into the tools, interfaces, and actions people already take every day. Sensitivity labels apply automatically, DLP policies run in the background, permissions inherit cleanly, and environment policies activate from the moment an agent or workspace is created. When governance becomes invisible, compliance becomes the default behavior.

2. **Create Governance Zones That Match Risk**

   Not all agent activity carries the same level of risk, so governance shouldn't treat all scenarios equally. The most effective execution model uses zoning – structured spaces that match the level of data sensitivity, autonomy, and operational impact of an agent. A Green Zone supports experimentation without fear, a Yellow Zone adds guardrails for semi-sensitive workflows, and a Red Zone enforces strict oversight for mission-critical or regulated data. This approach protects your tenant and keeps teams moving fast.

3. **Standardize the Agent Life Cycle**

Consistency is the backbone of operational governance, and agents need the same life cycle discipline we apply to software, APIs, and automation. A standard agent life cycle with stages like draft, validate, pilot, deploy, monitor, review/retire – removes ambiguity and prevents "shadow agents" from quietly expanding without oversight. When every agent follows the same path, approvals become predictable, quality becomes measurable, and governance becomes a repeatable rhythm rather than a firefight.

4. **Align People, Processes, and Platforms**

I've watched governance fail when people, processes, and platforms aren't moving in sync. People should define roles and accountability, processes outline how decisions flow, and platforms enforce rules and policies at scale. Without this alignment, governance becomes fragmented – too many owners, unclear workflows, or tools that enforce policies nobody understands. Real execution happens when each layer reinforces the other and no step depends purely on human memory.

5. **Replace One-Time Reviews with Continuous Monitoring**

Periodic reviews aren't enough for AI systems that evolve through usage, data exposure, and new actions. Governance must shift from one-time "checkpoint approvals" to continuous telemetry, showing real-time signals about usage, drift, and data exposure. This turns governance into an ongoing system of awareness rather than a scheduled audit, ensuring issues are caught early – before an agent scales or a risk escalates.

6. **Bake Governance into Culture, Not Just Controls**

Even perfect technical controls can fail if the people using the systems don't understand the why behind them. Governance becomes sustainable when it's part of the organization's cultural fabric – when teams instinctively escalate concerns, follow responsible AI patterns, and understand what safe automation looks like.

Controls provide protection; culture provides continuity. Together, they create an environment where AI can scale responsibly.

7. **Start Small, Scale Fast**

I've seen the fastest path to large-scale governance is disciplined iteration, not sweeping enterprise programs. Start with one business unit, a handful of agents, a single pipeline, and one governance pattern. Prove the model, tune it, remove friction, and then scale horizontally across teams. This approach de-risks adoption while building confidence, clarity, and momentum – allowing the organization to scale AI safely without slowing down innovation.

GPSR Compliance
The European Union's (EU) General Product Safety Regulation (GPSR) is a set
of rules that requires consumer products to be safe and our obligations to
ensure this.

If you have any concerns about our products, you can contact us on

ProductSafety@springernature.com

In case Publisher is established outside the EU, the EU authorized
representative is:

Springer Nature Customer Service Center GmbH
Europaplatz 3
69115 Heidelberg, Germany